How To Draw Skulls For Beginners

Draw Skulls Step By Step Guided Book

By Gala Publication

Published By:

Gala Publication

ISBN-13 : 978-1515169239
ISBN-10: 1515169235

©Copyright 2015 – Gala Publication

Table of Contents

Deer Skull

Step 1

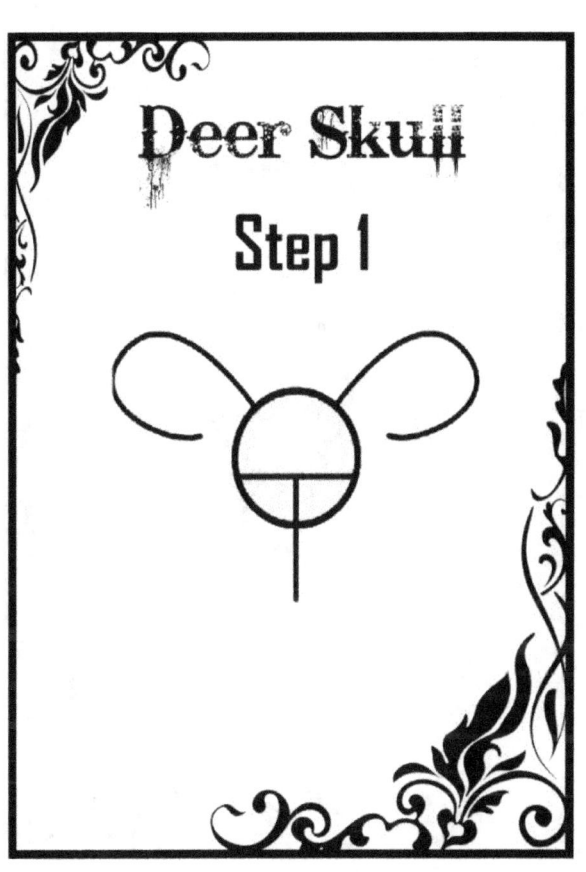

Step 2

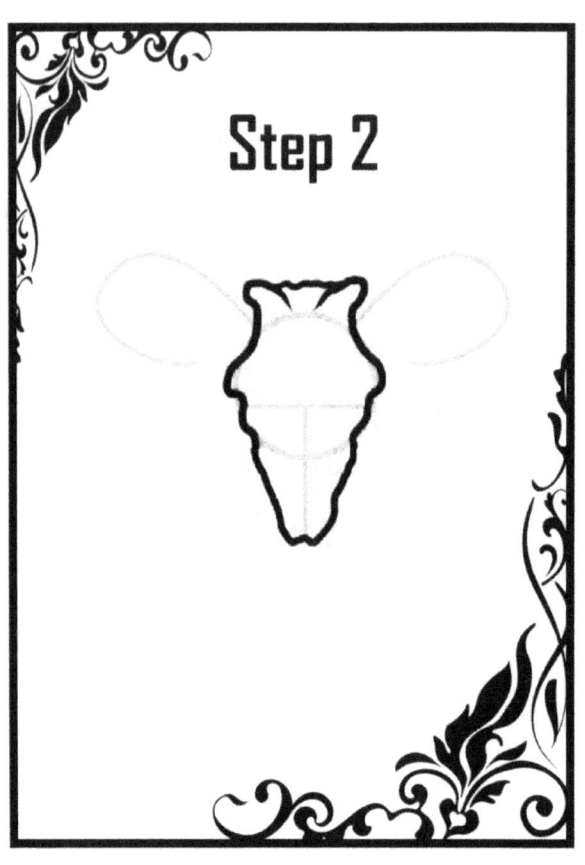

Step 3

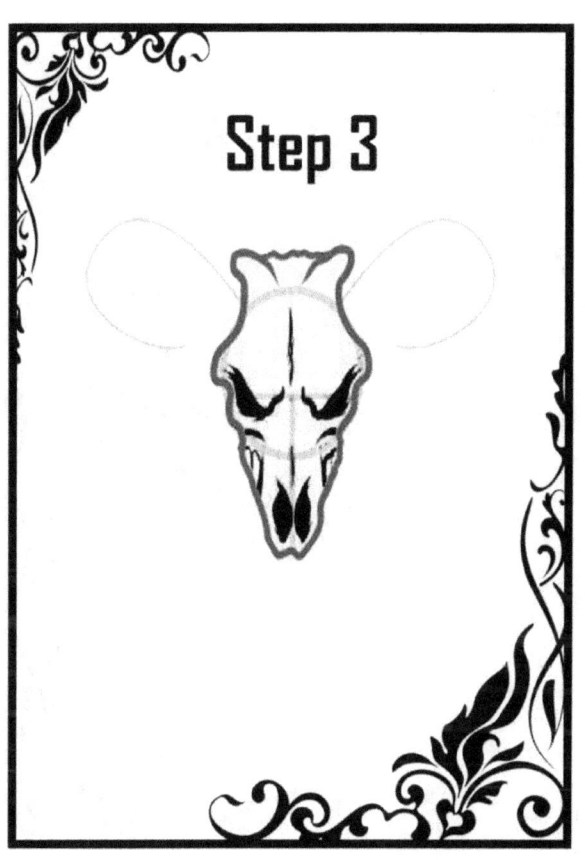

Step 4

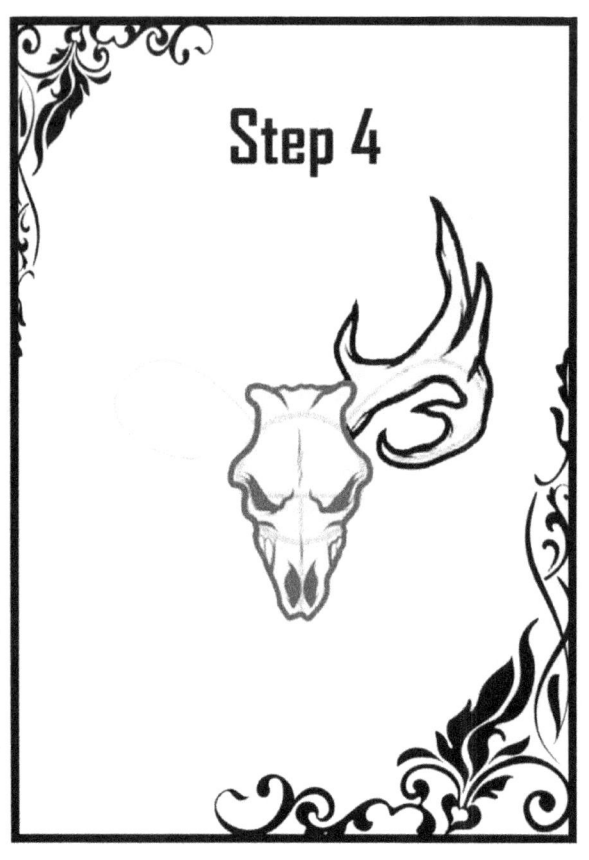

Step 5

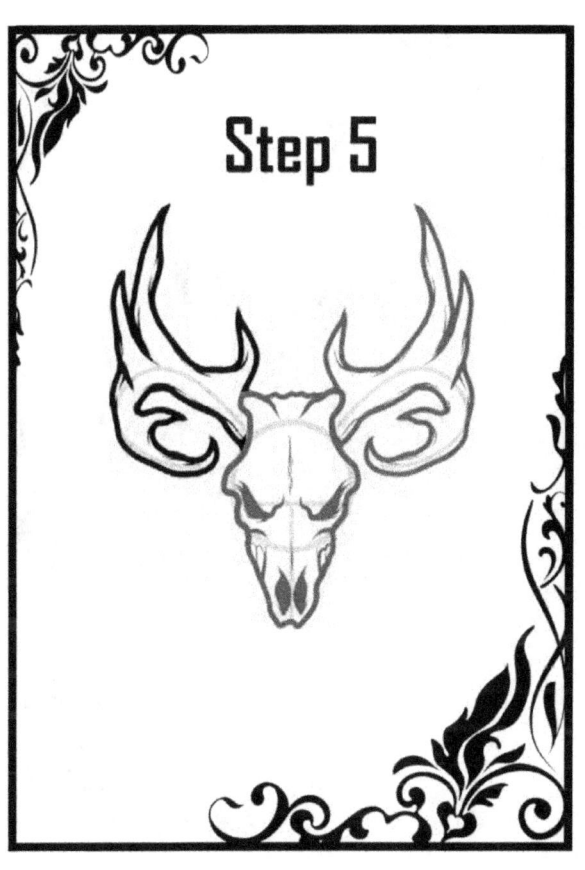

Step 6

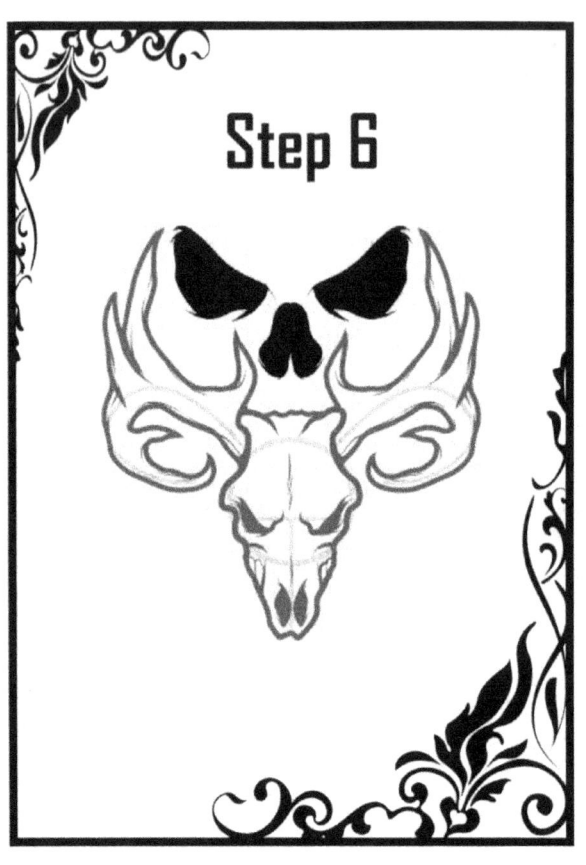

Step 7

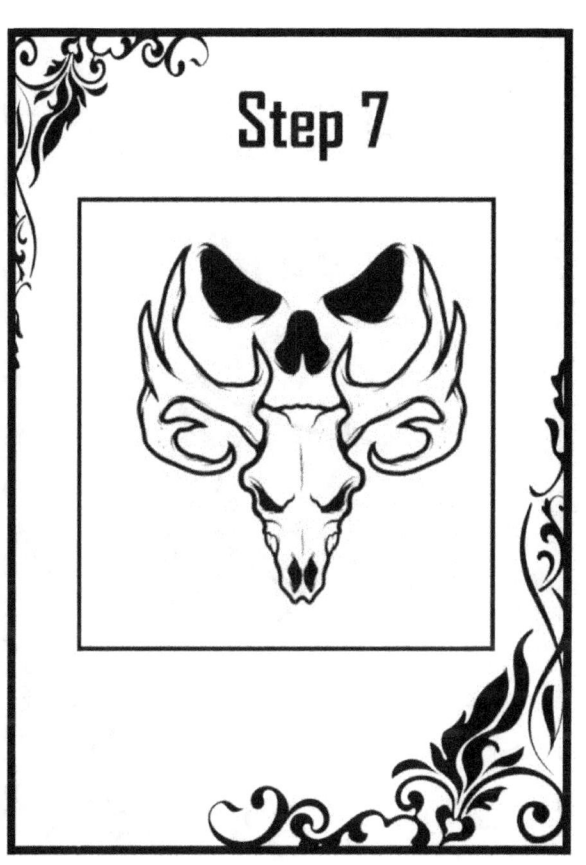

Grim Reaper

Step 1

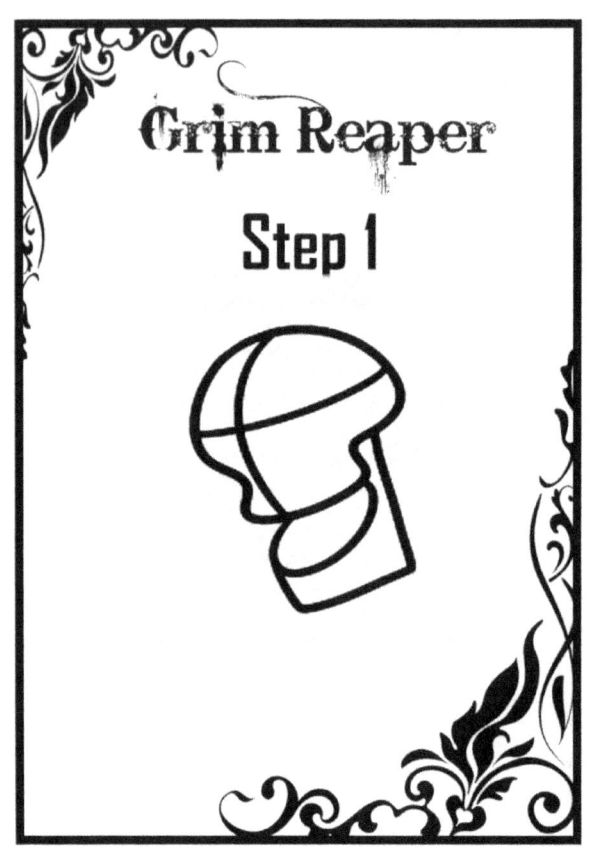

Step 2

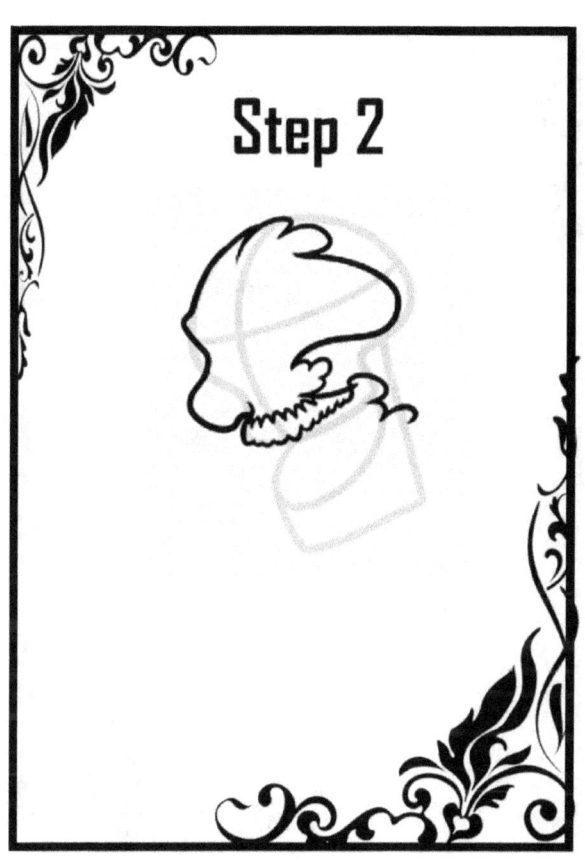

Step 3

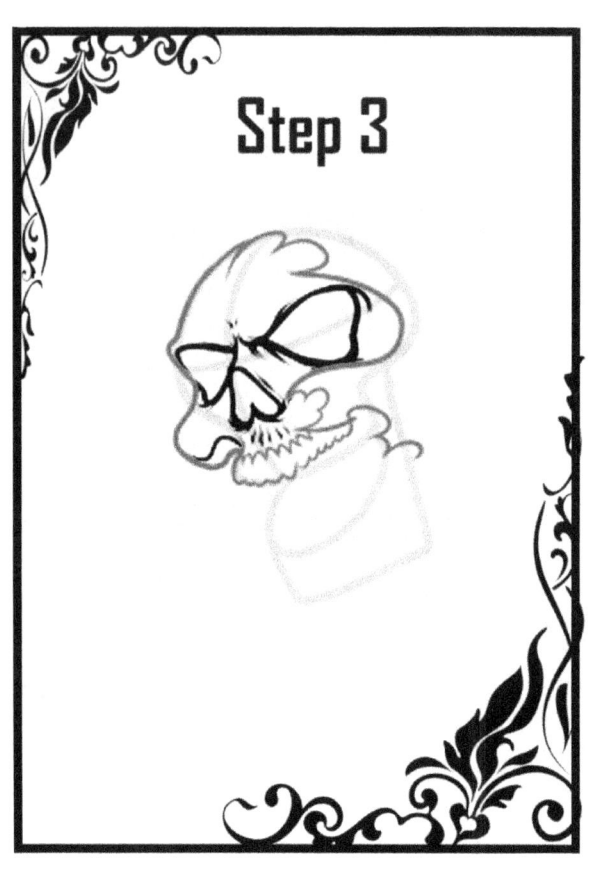

Step 4

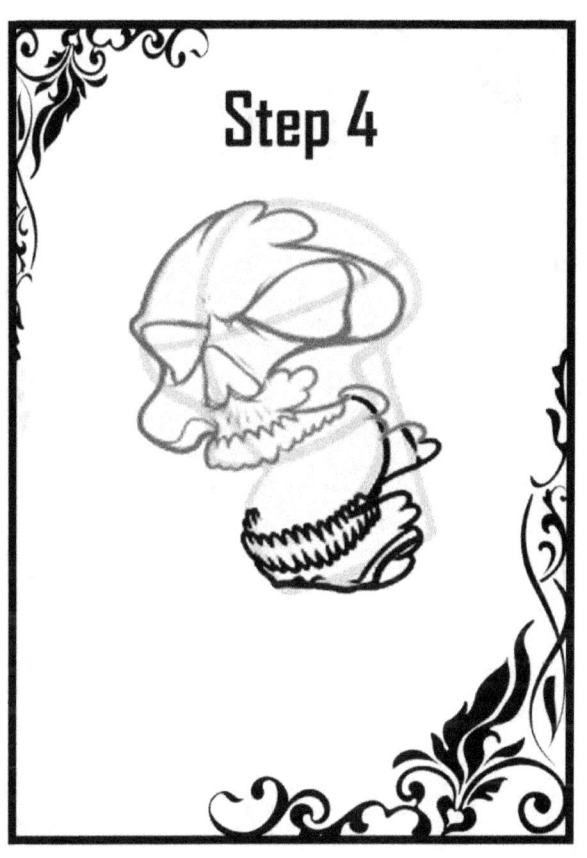

Step 5

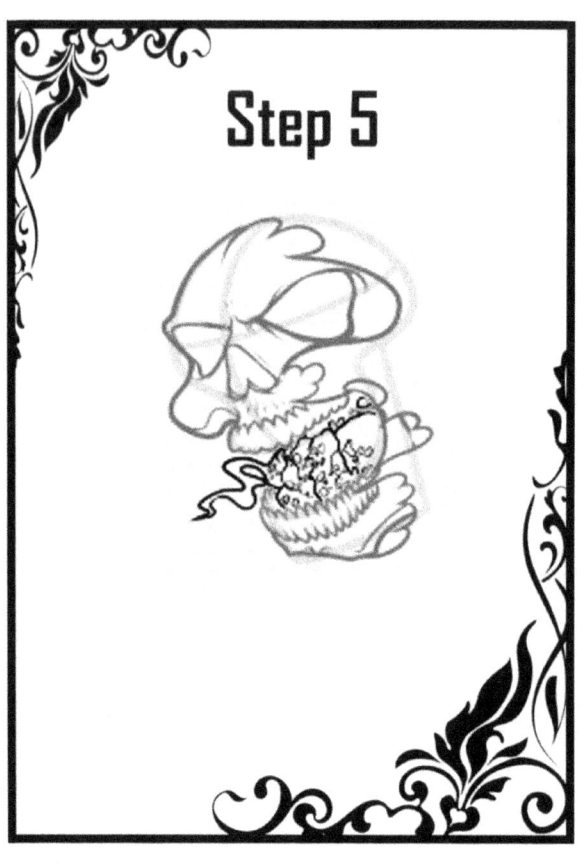

Step 6

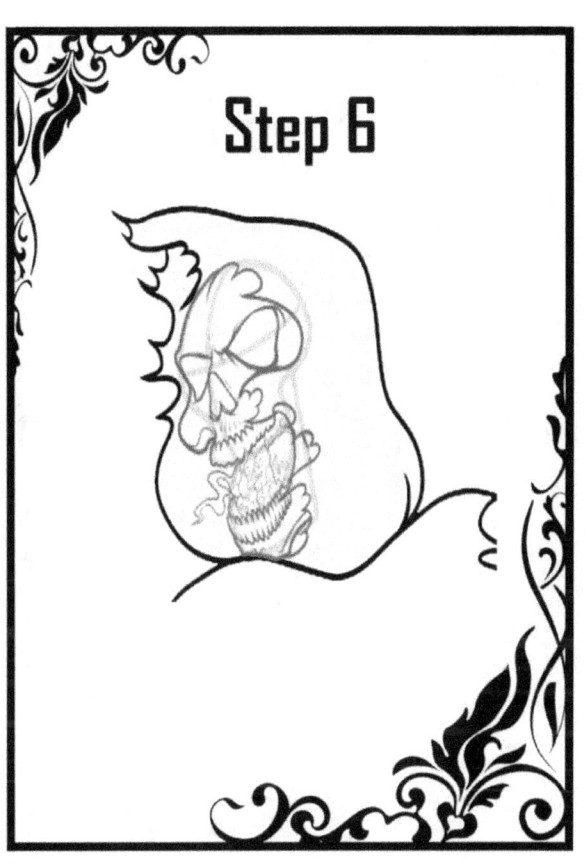

Step 7

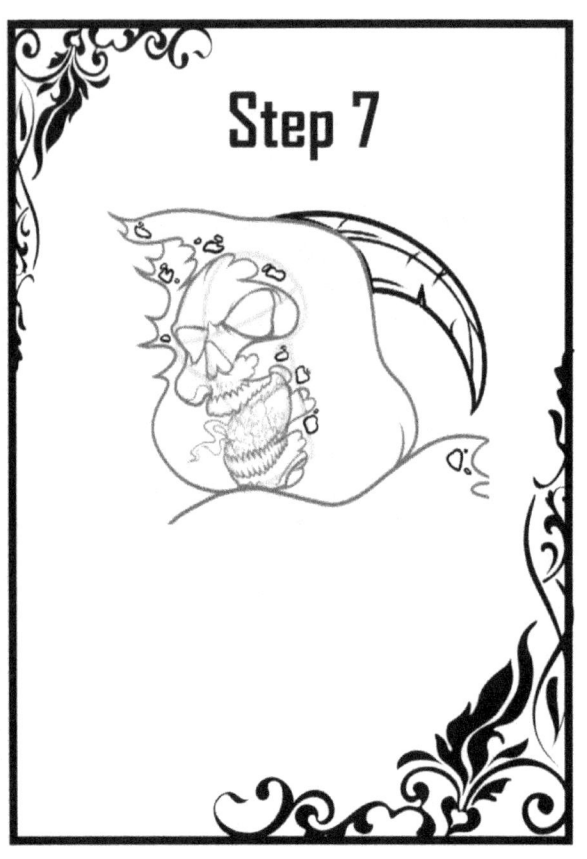

Step 8

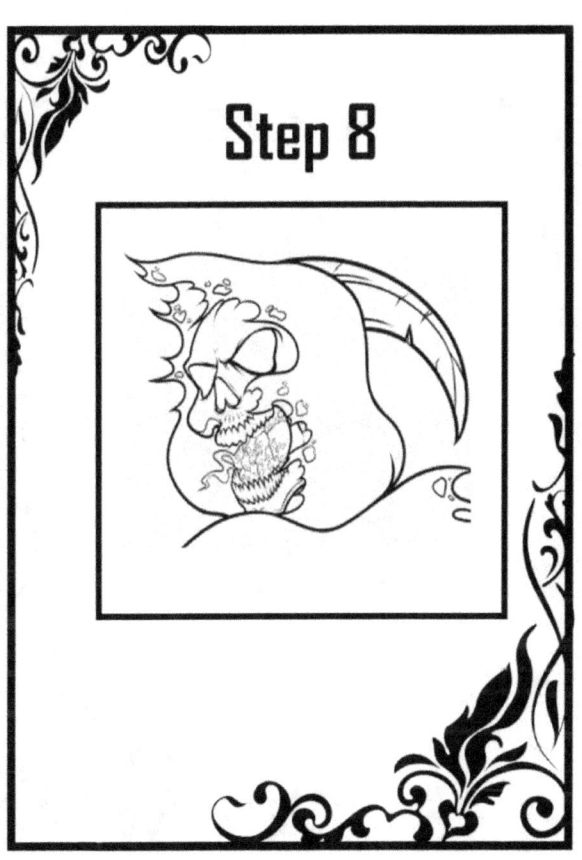

octopus

Step 1

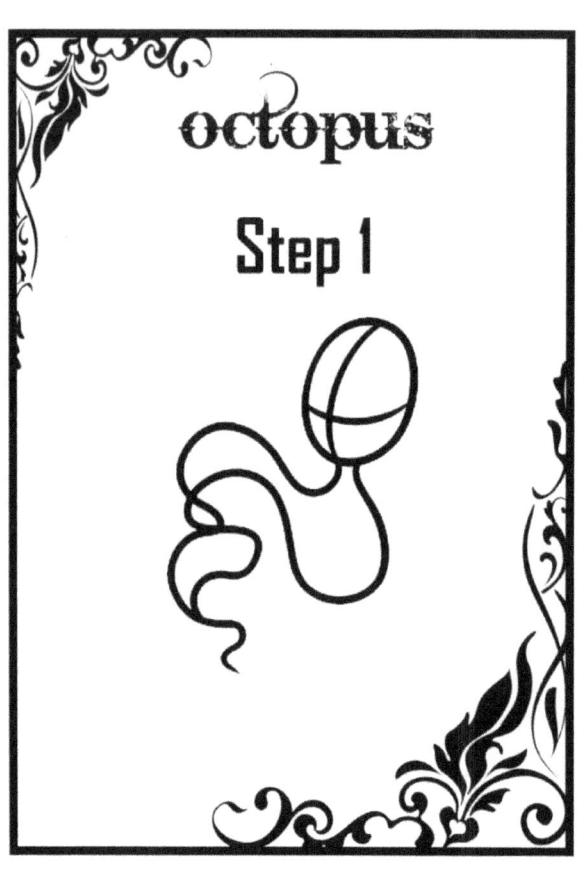

Step 2

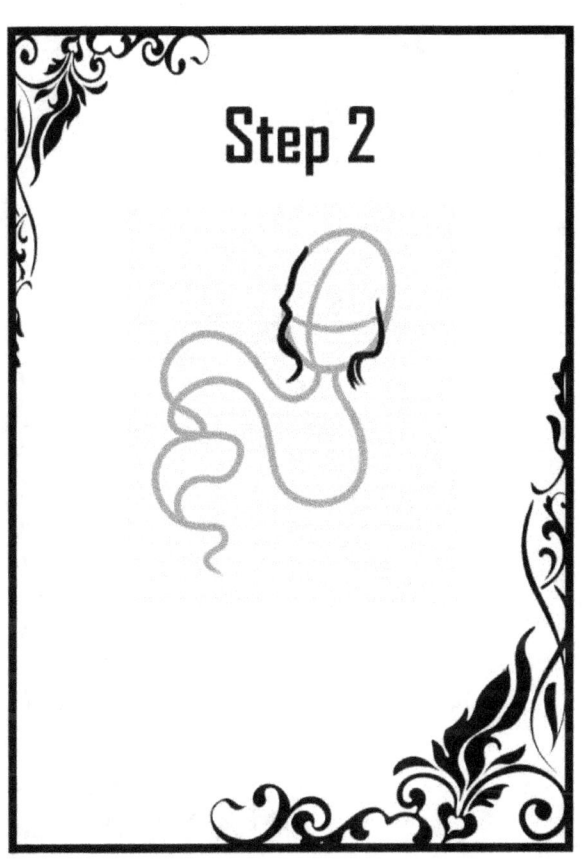

Step 3

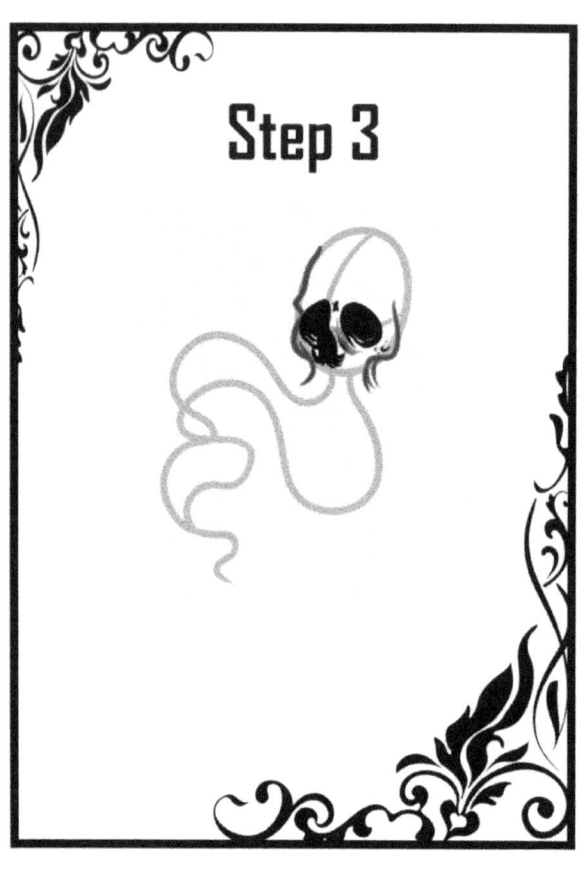

Step 4

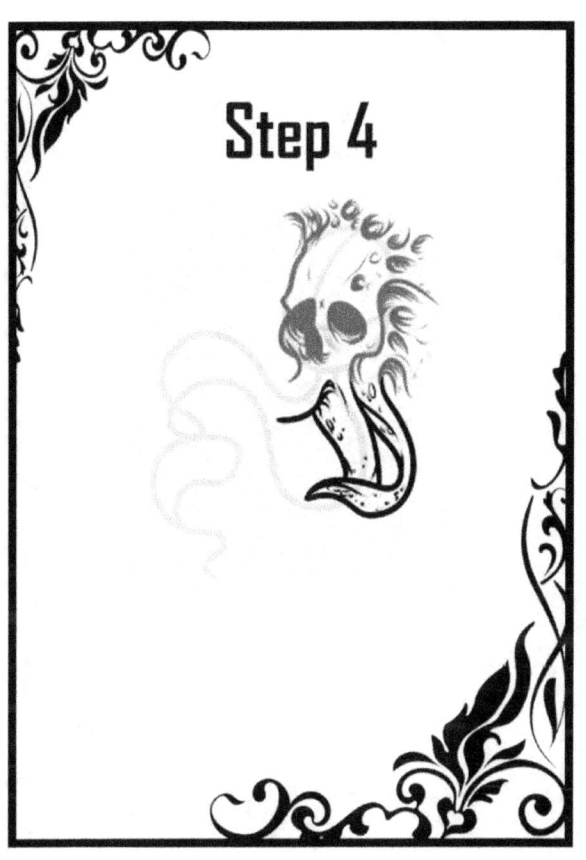

Step 5

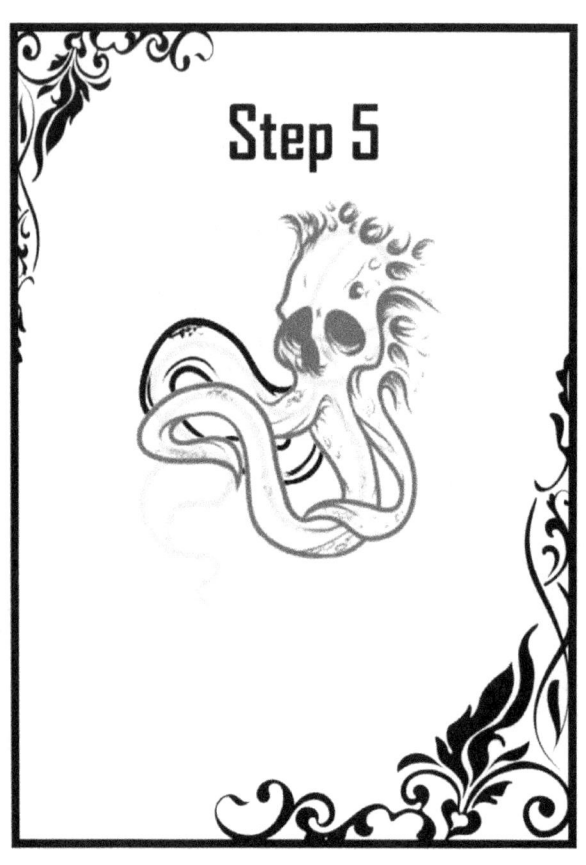

Step 6

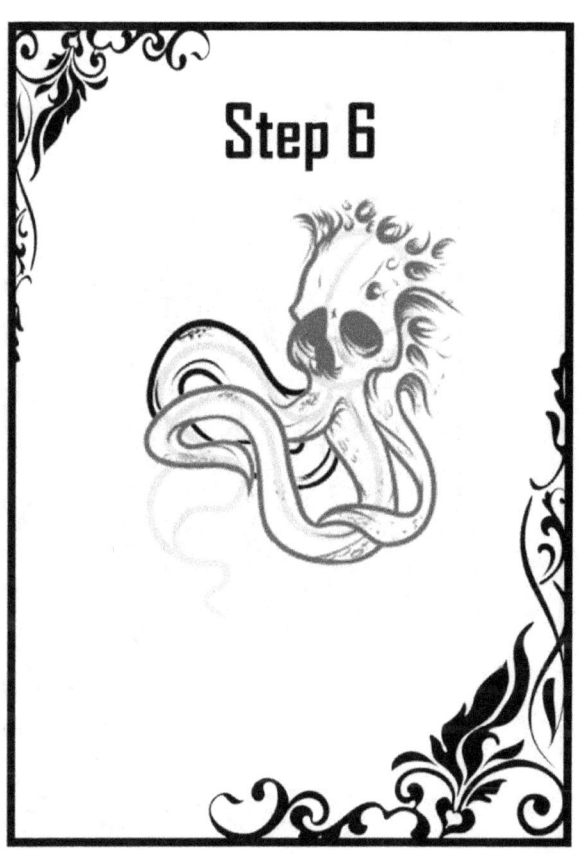

Step 7

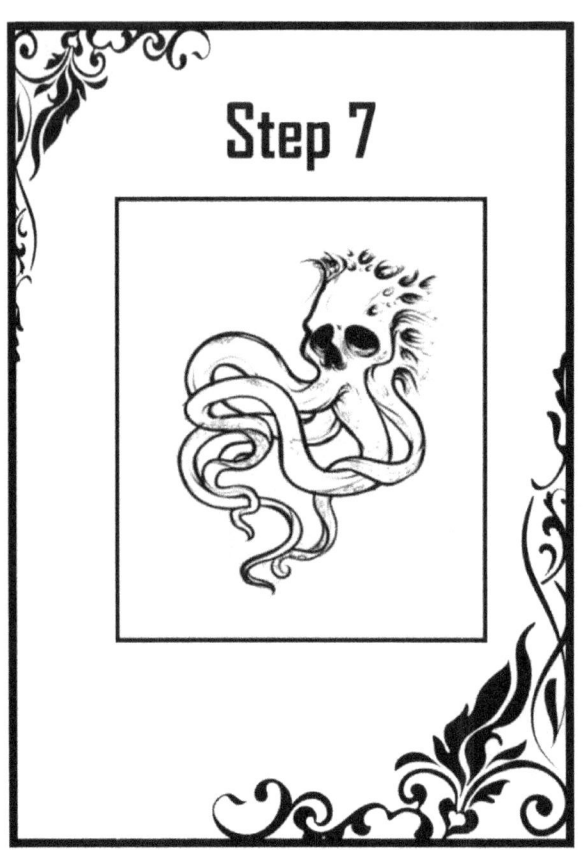

Owl

Step 1

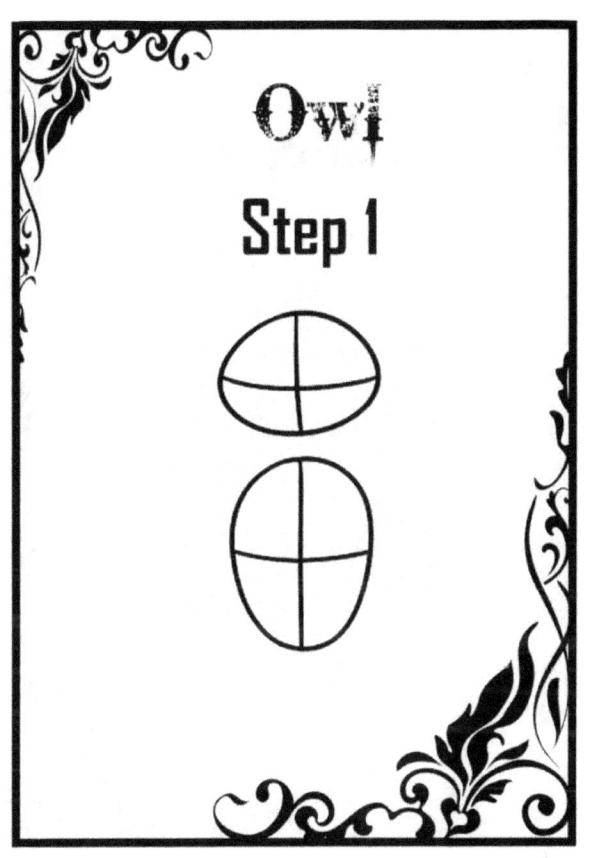

Step 2

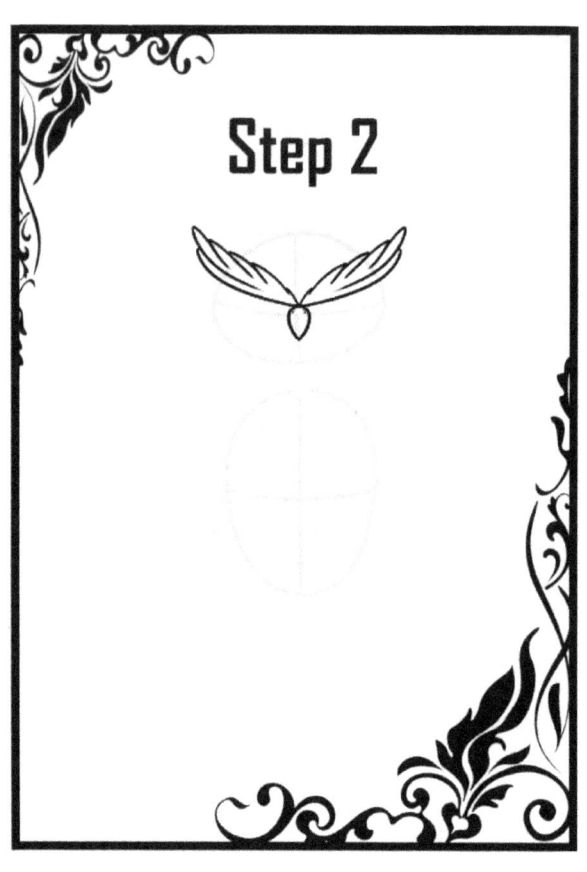

Step 3

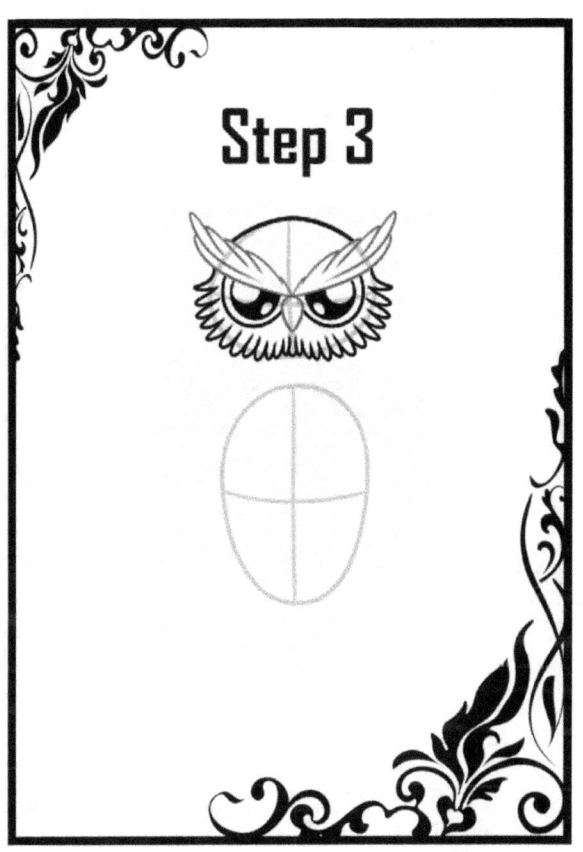

Step 4

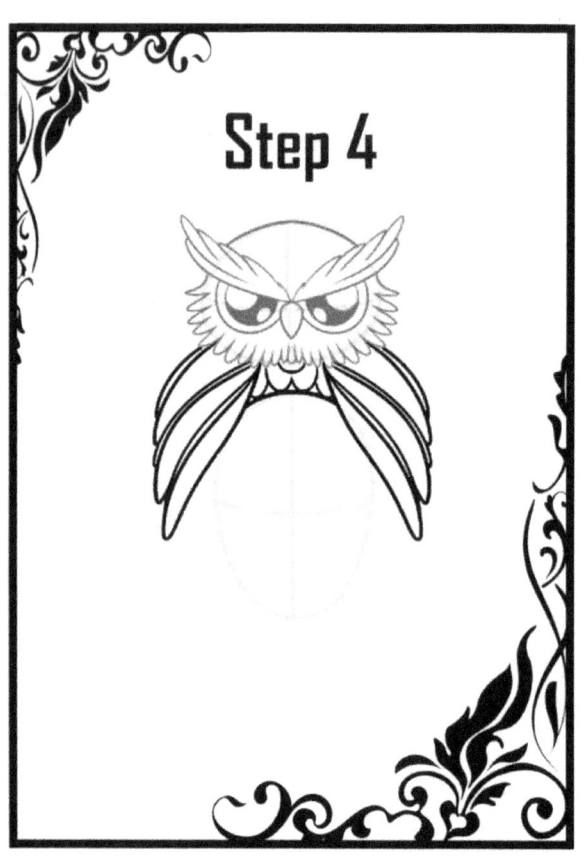

Step 5

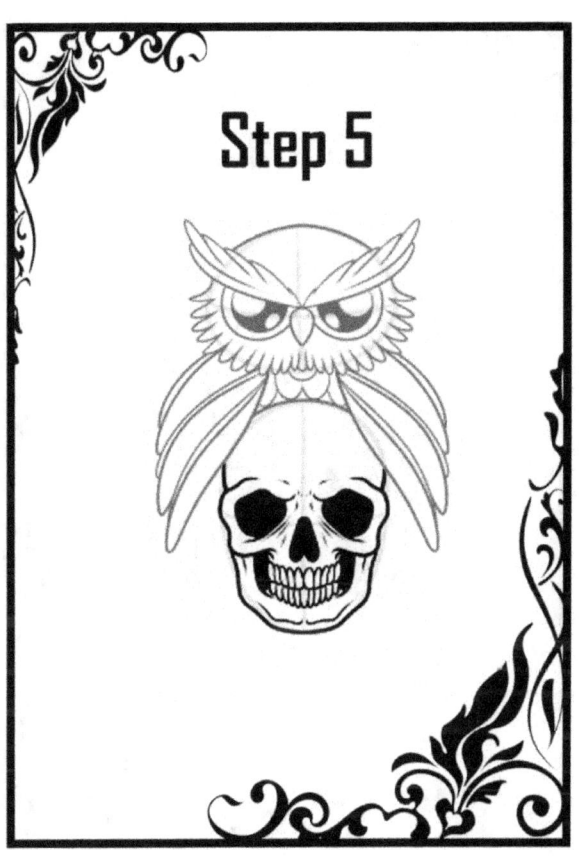

Step 6

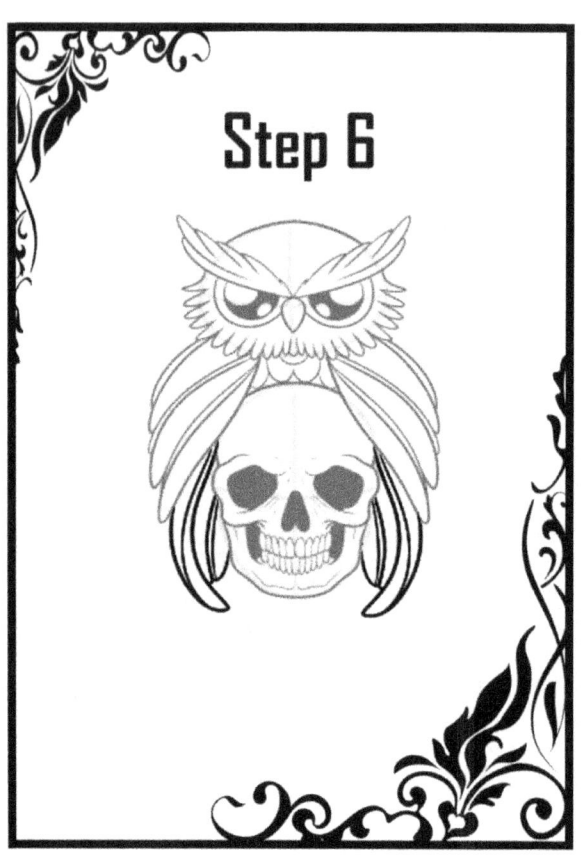

Step 7

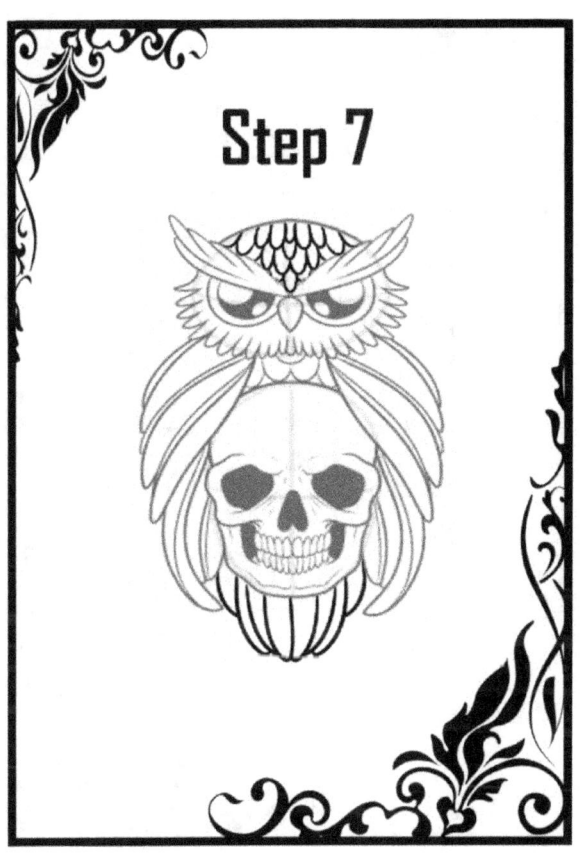

Step 8

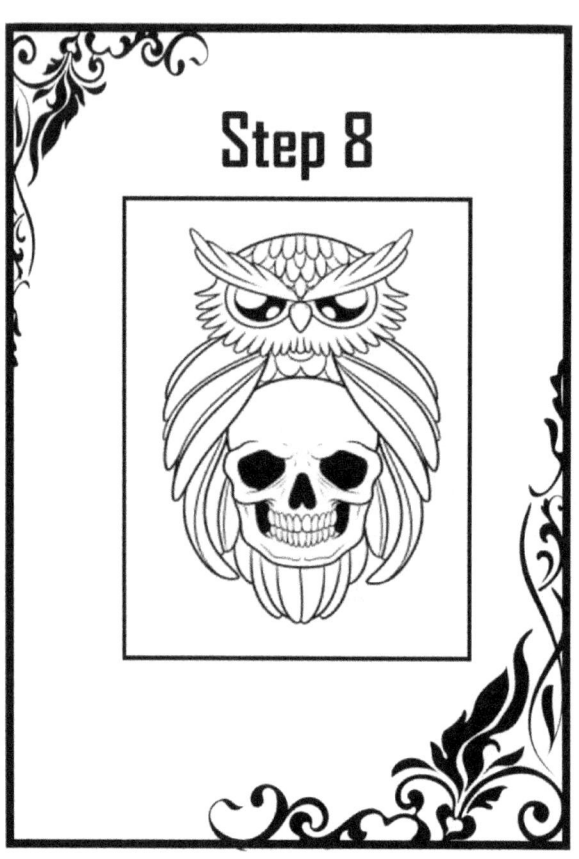

Skull and Snake

Step 1

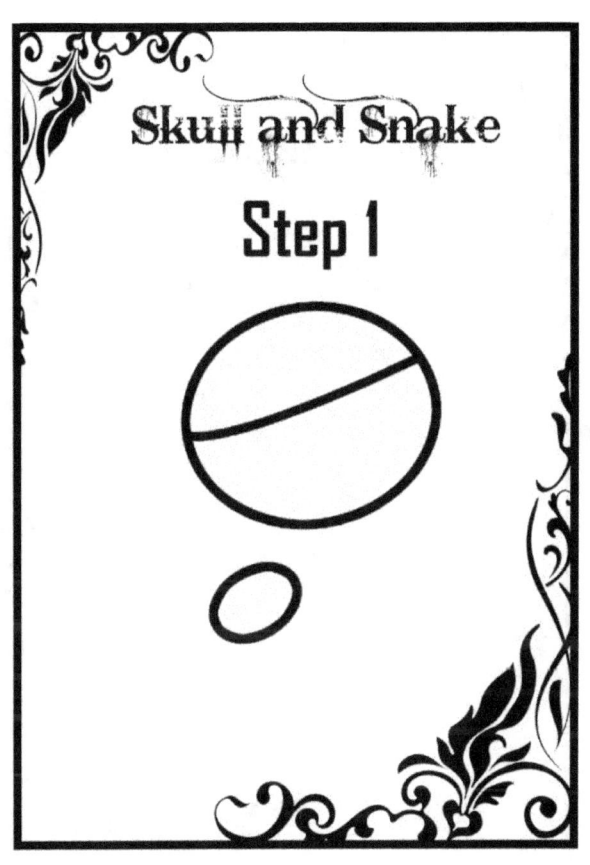

Step 2

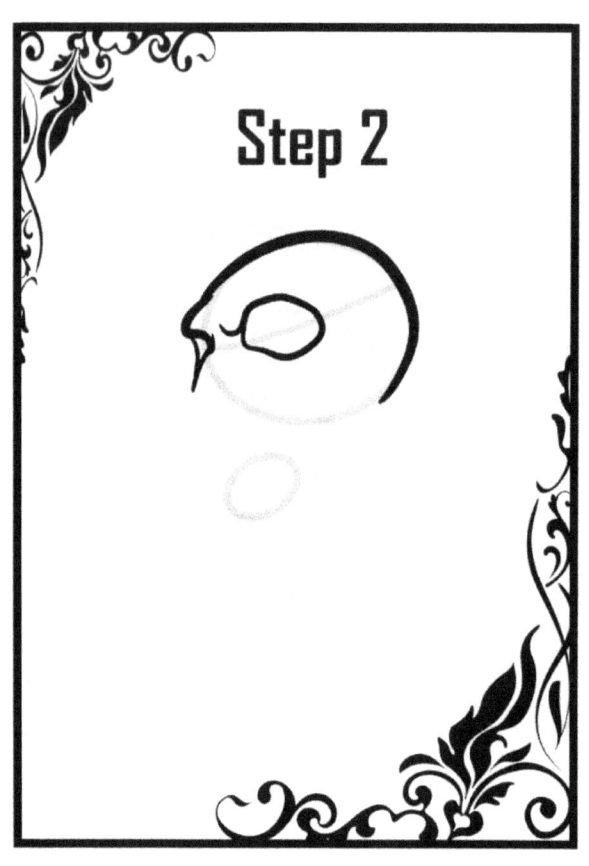

Step 3

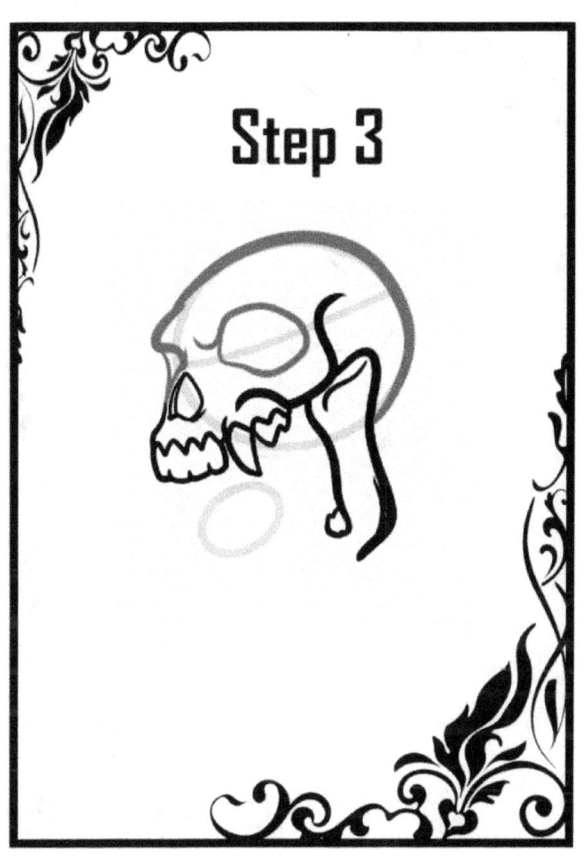

Step 4

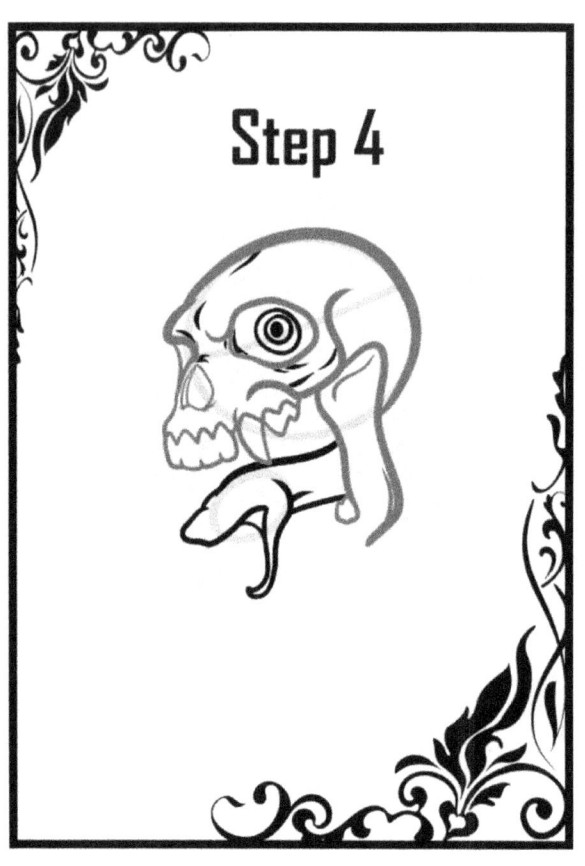

Step 5

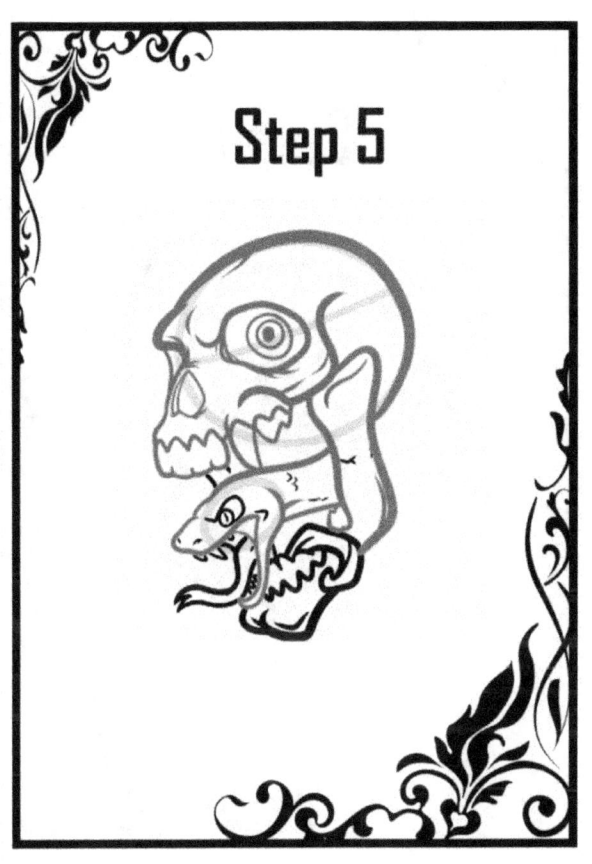

Step 6

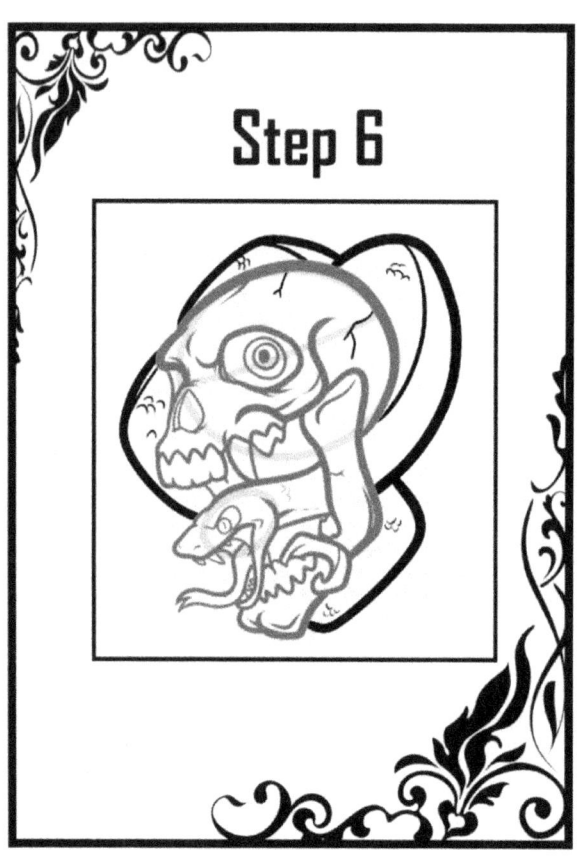

Spider Skull Tattoo

Step 1

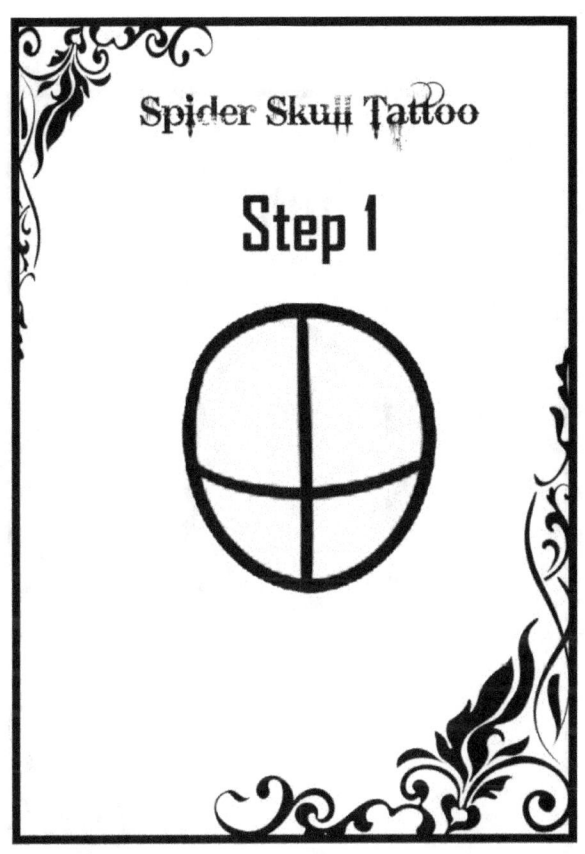

Step 2

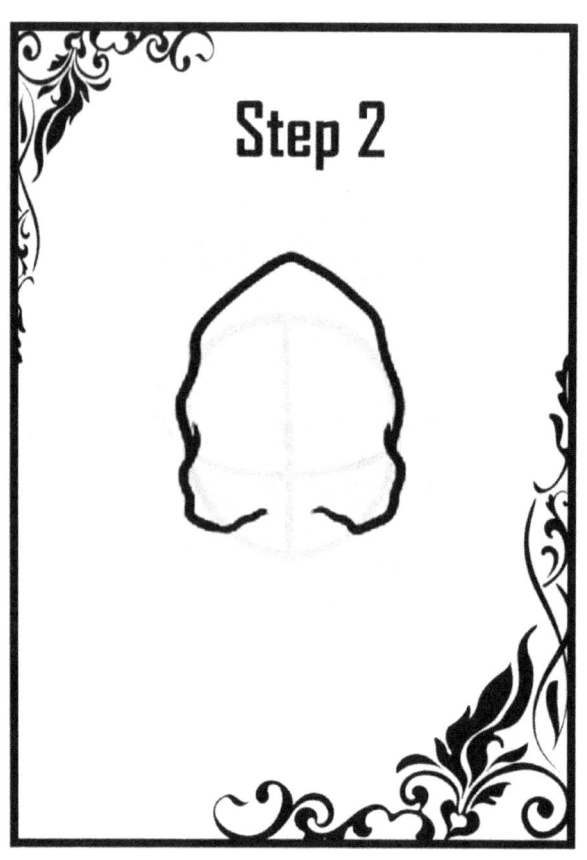

Step 3

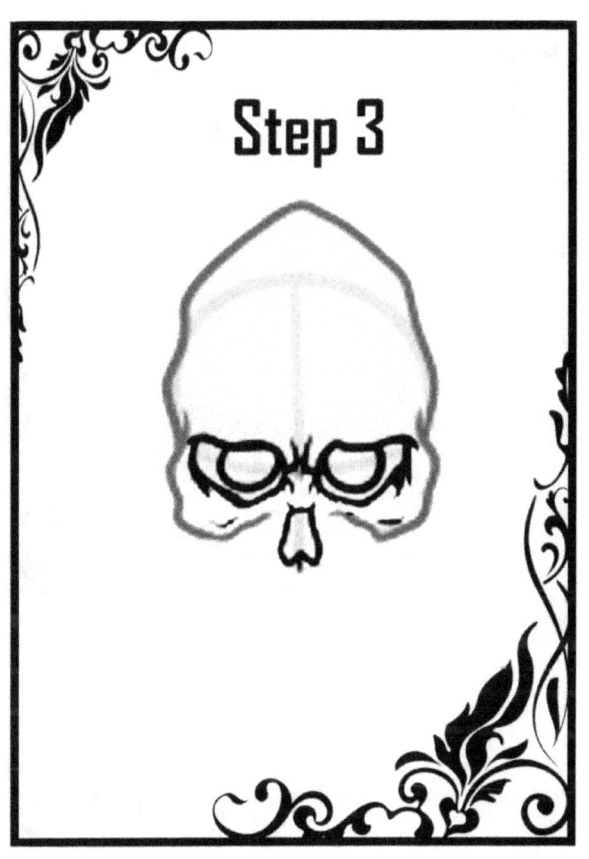

Step 4

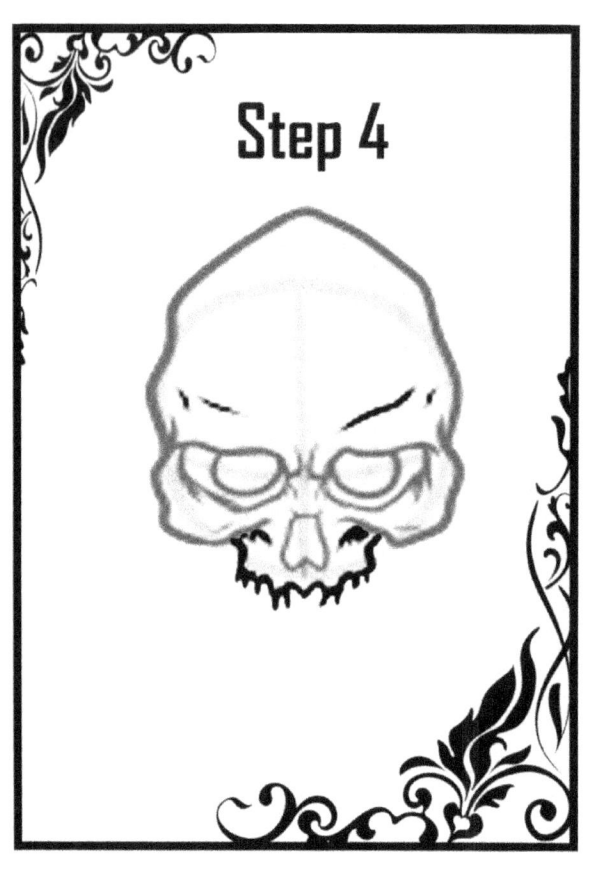

Step 5

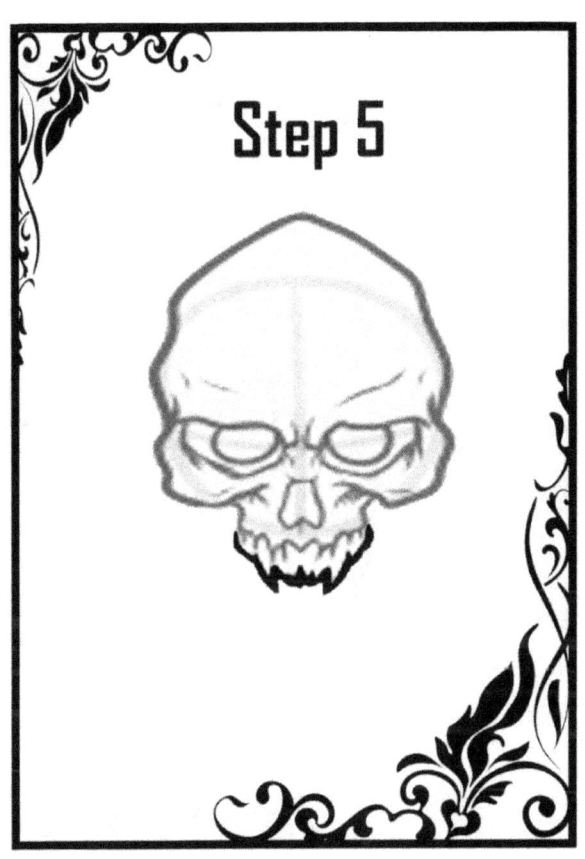

Step 6

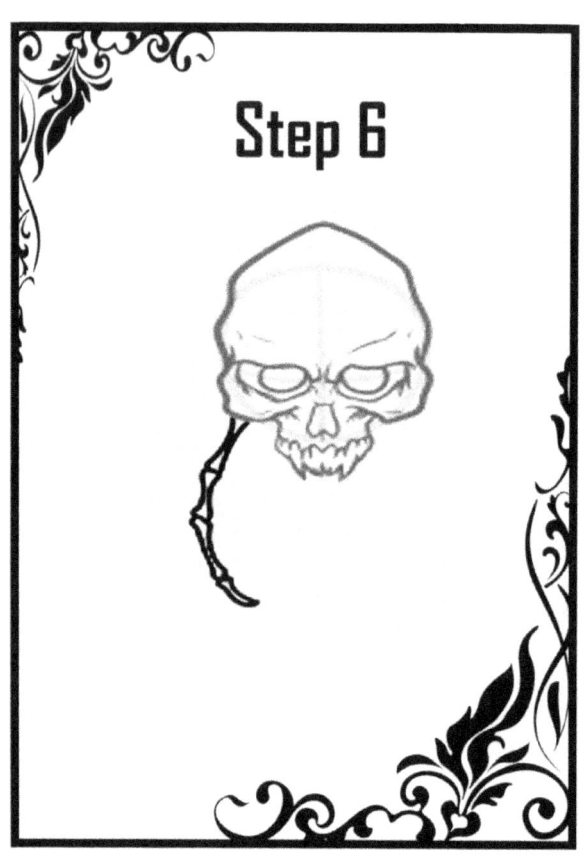

Step 7

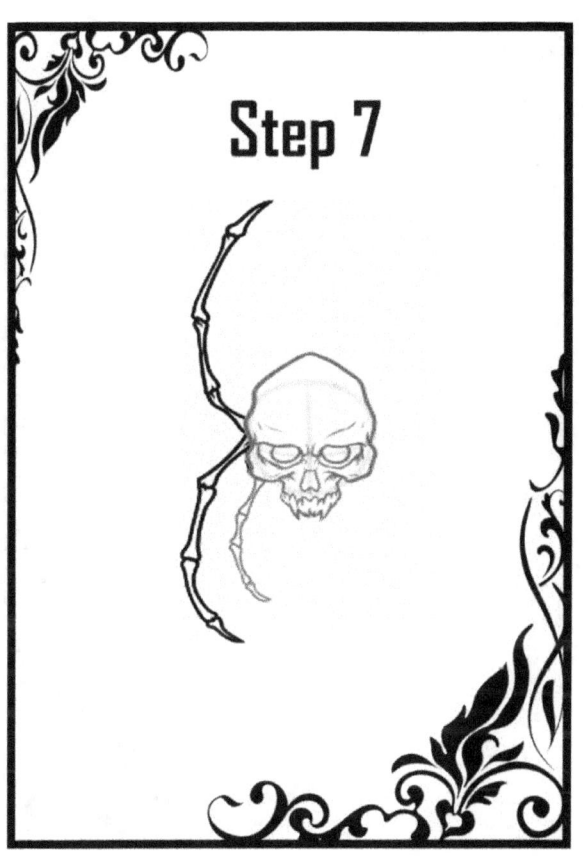

Step 8

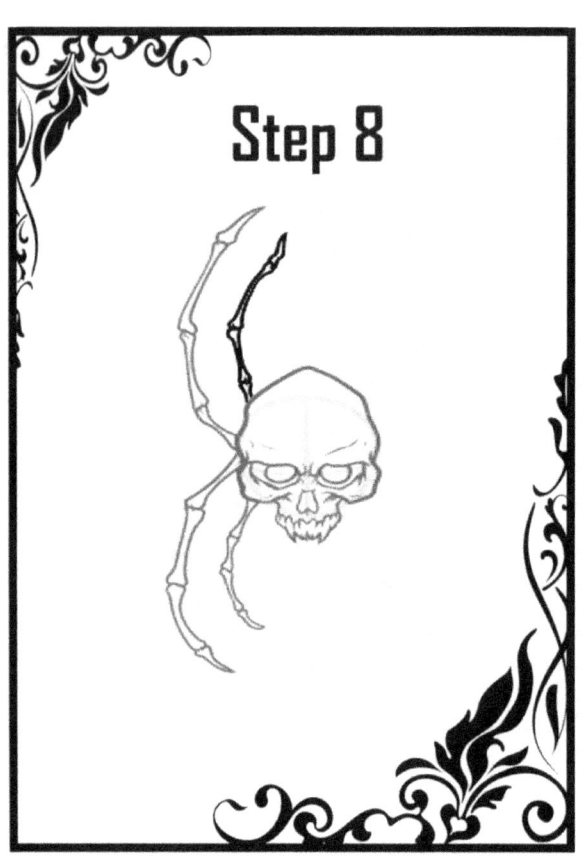

Step 9

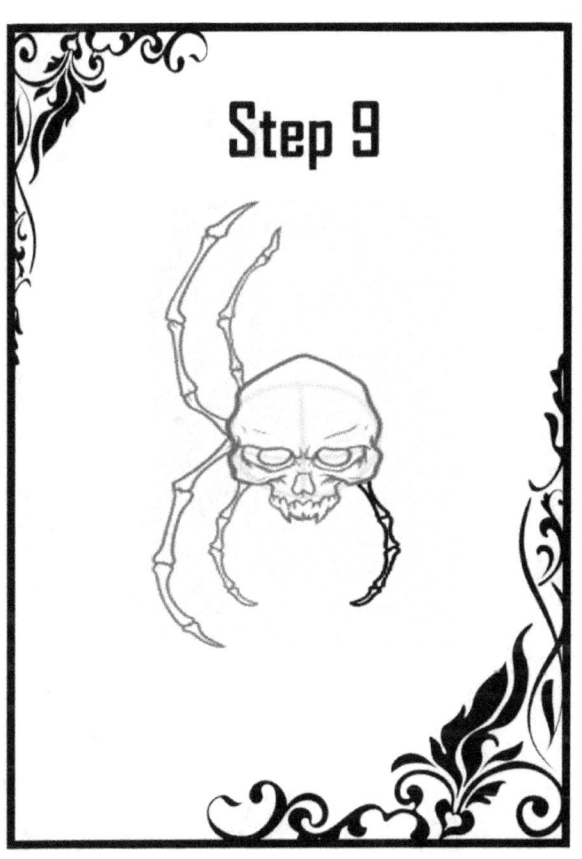

Step 10

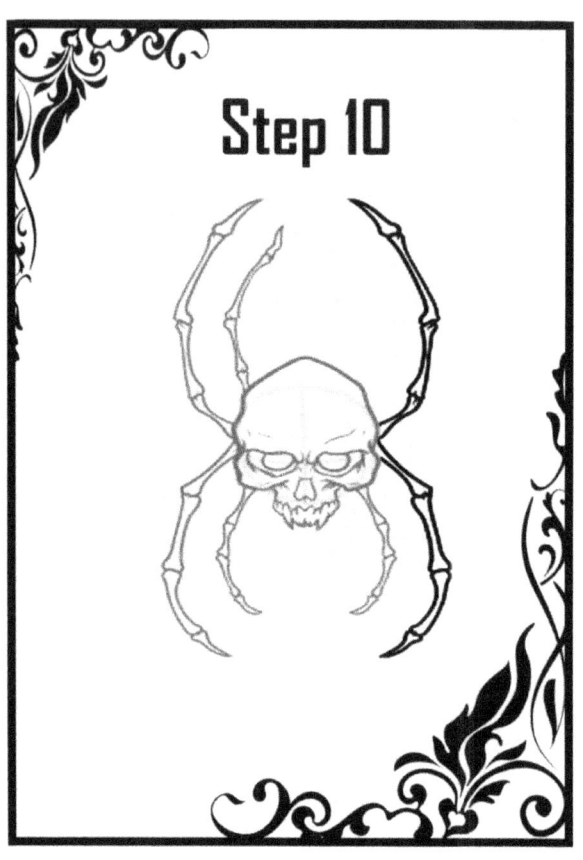

Step 11

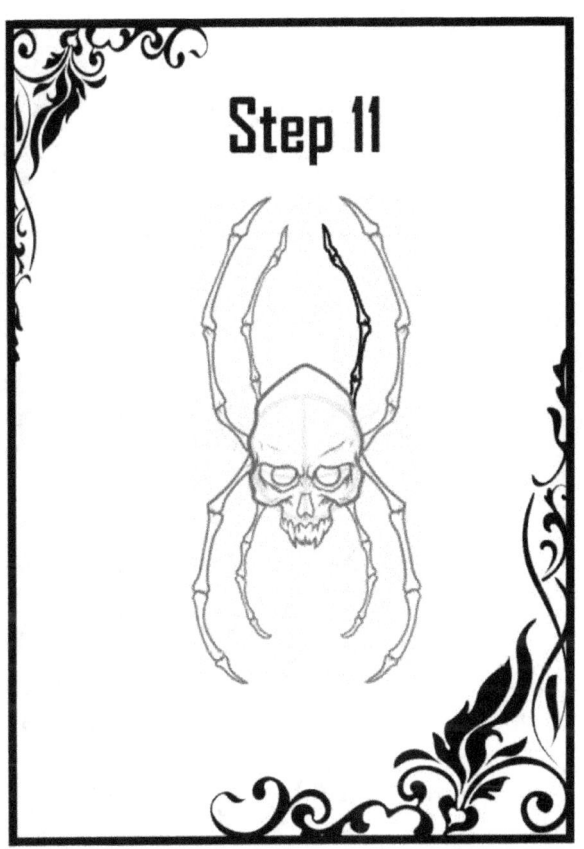

Step 12

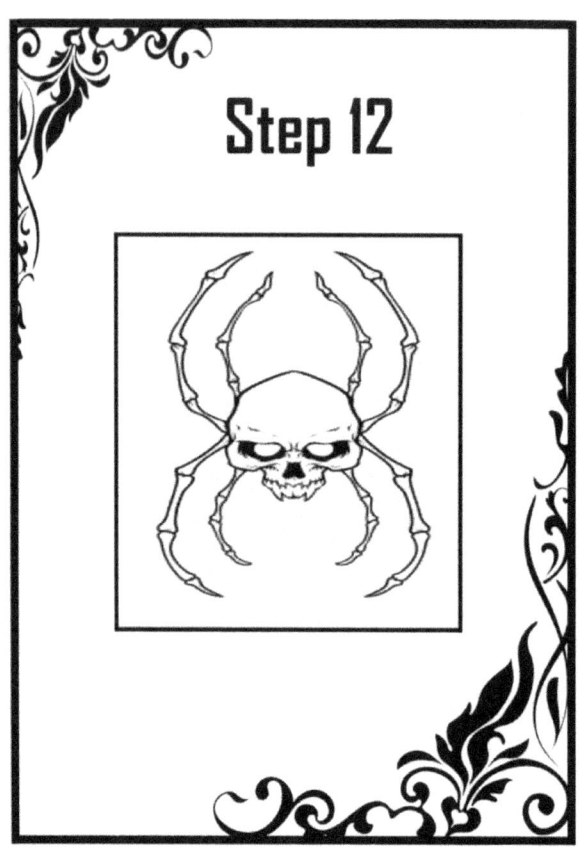

Skull Tattoos

Step 1

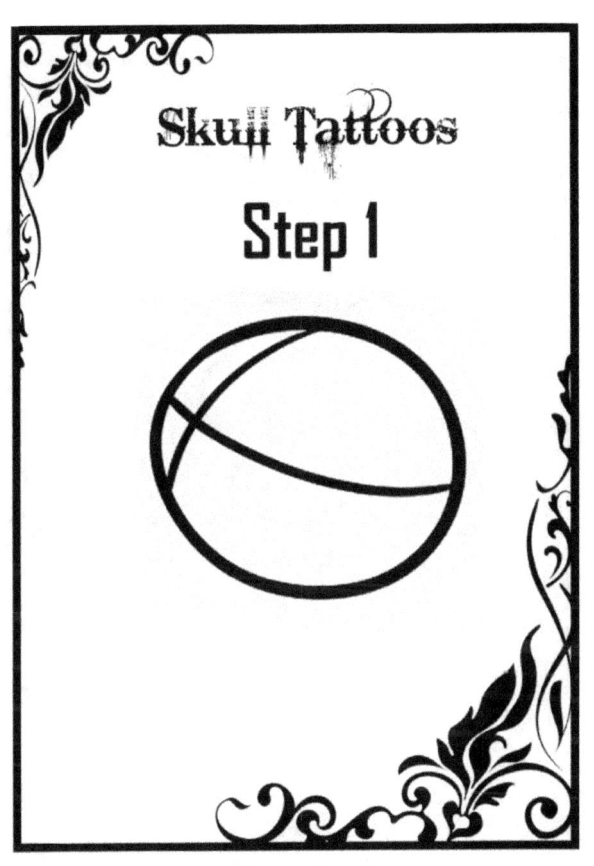

Step 2

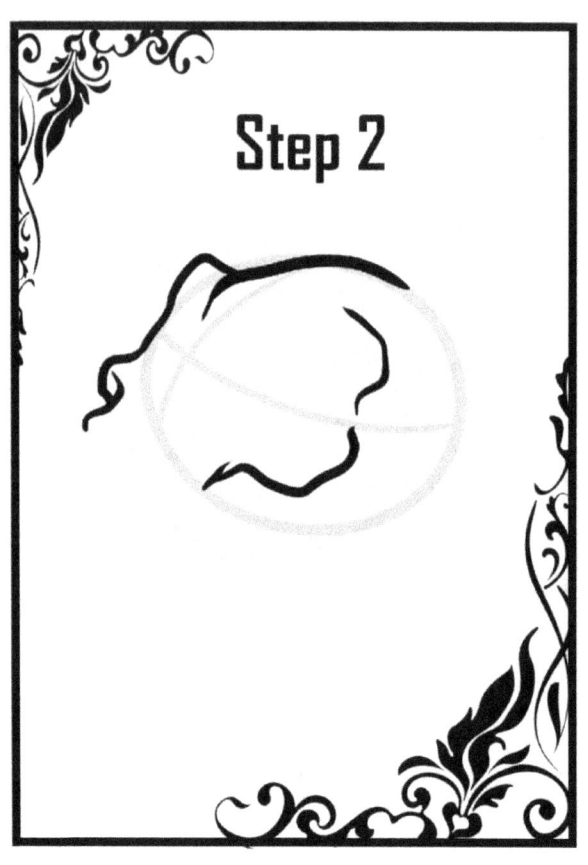

Step 3

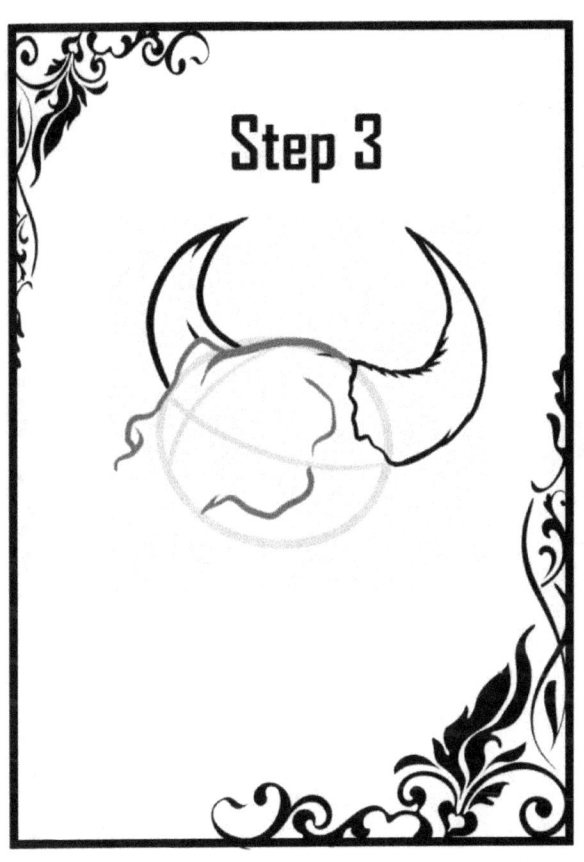

Step 4

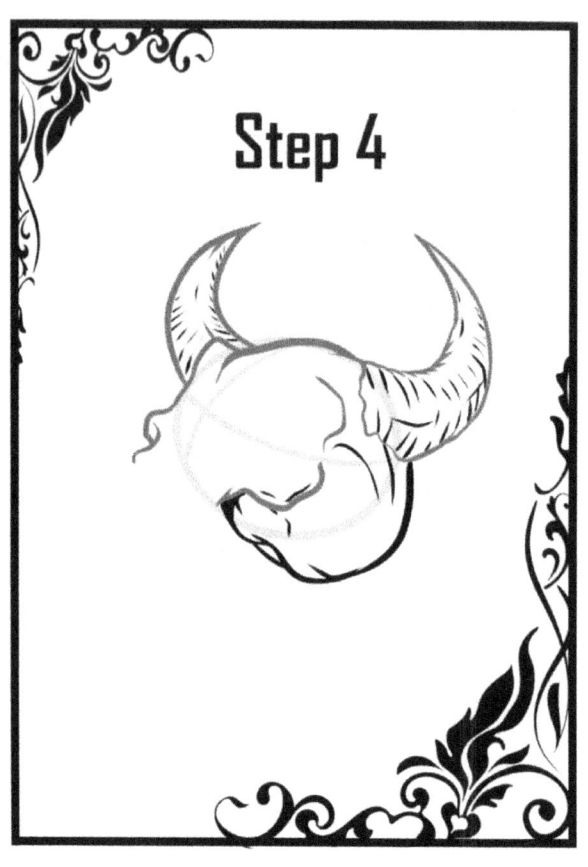

Step 5

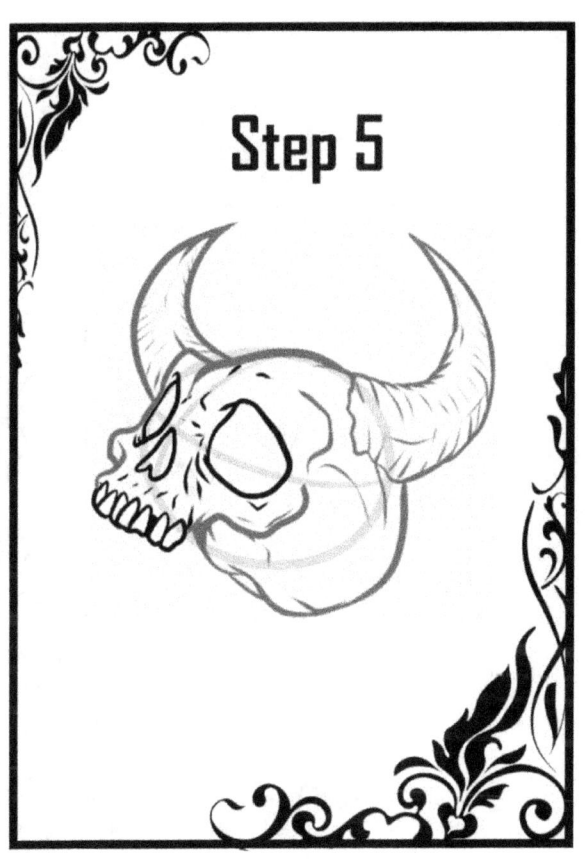

Step 6

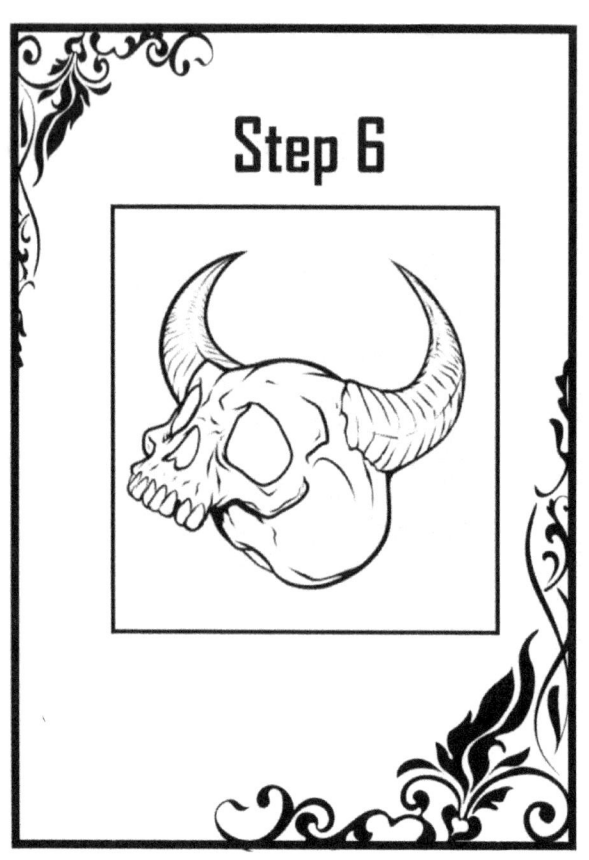

Time Tattoo

Step 1

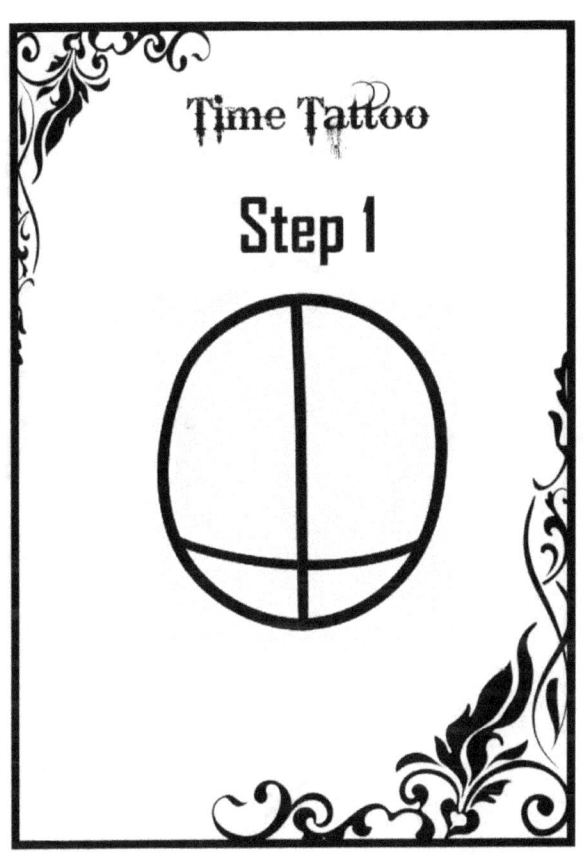

Step 2

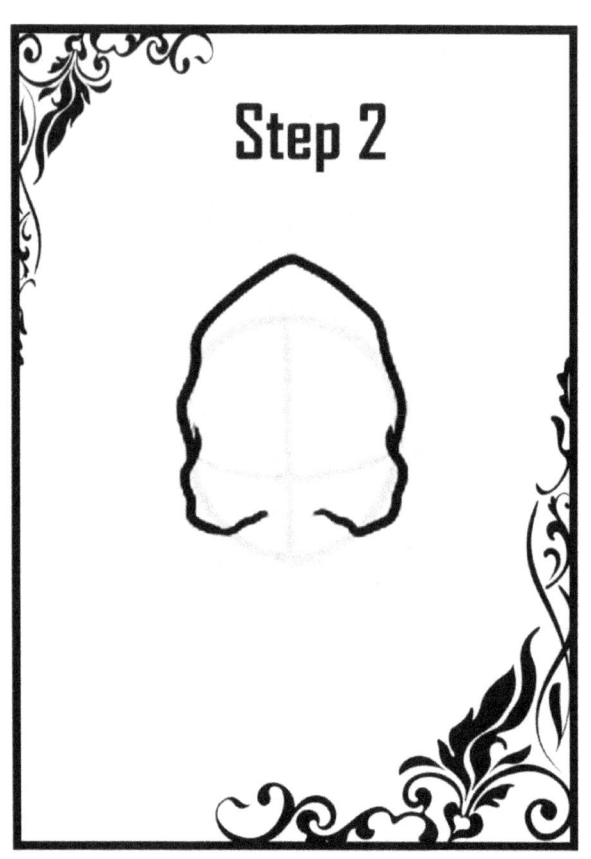

Step 3

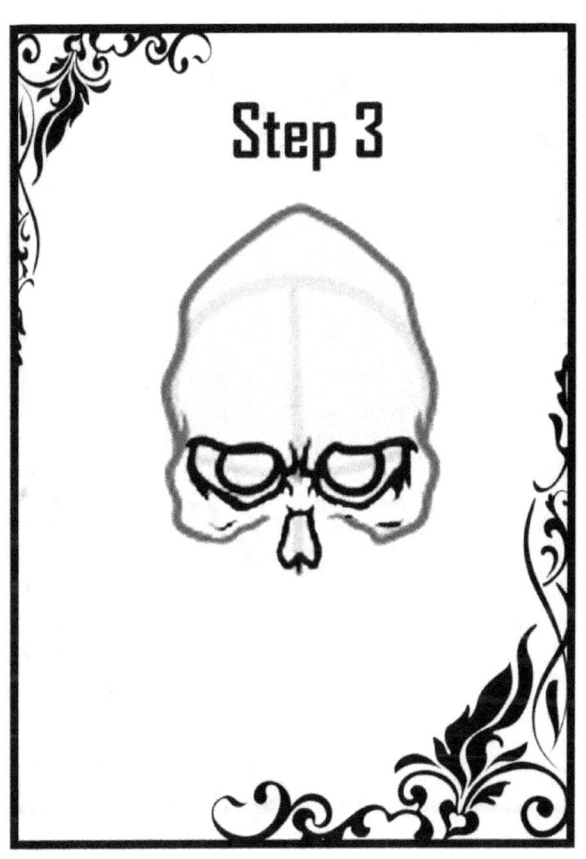

Step 4

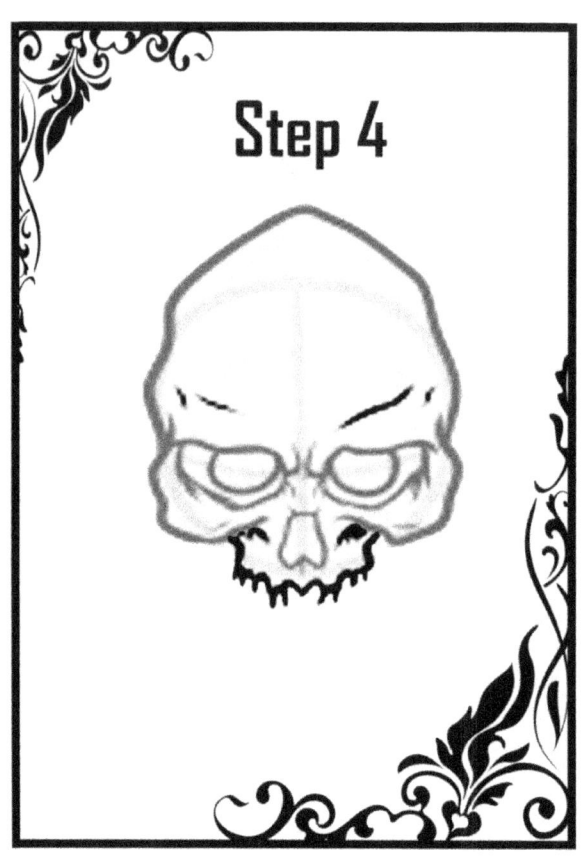

Step 5

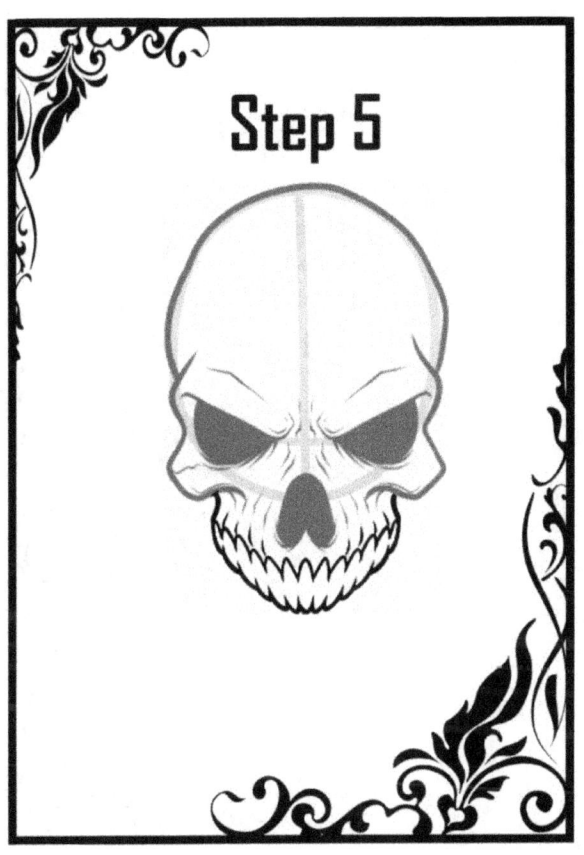

Step 6

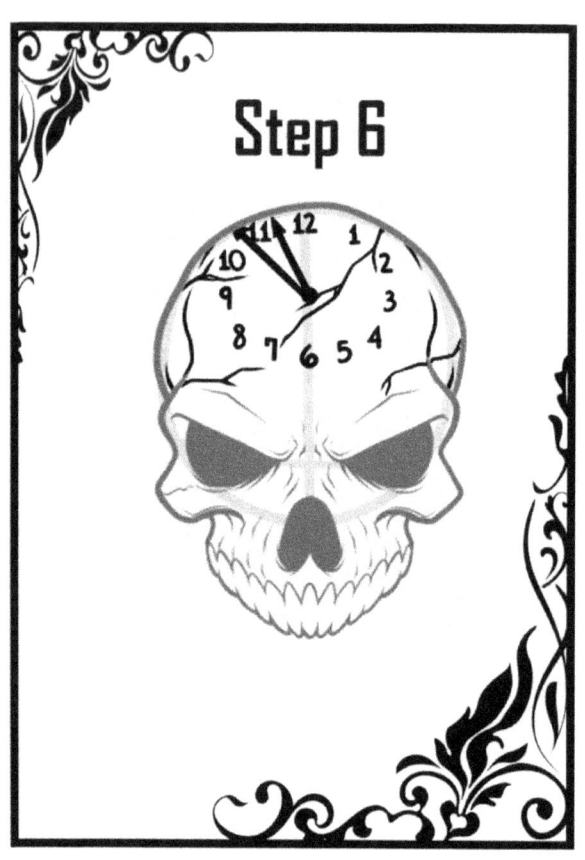

Step 7

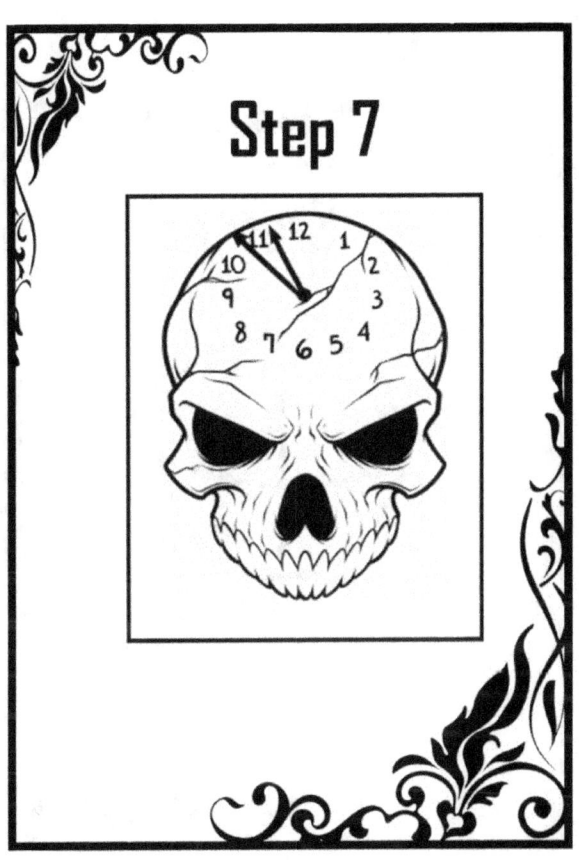

Traditional Skull

Step 1

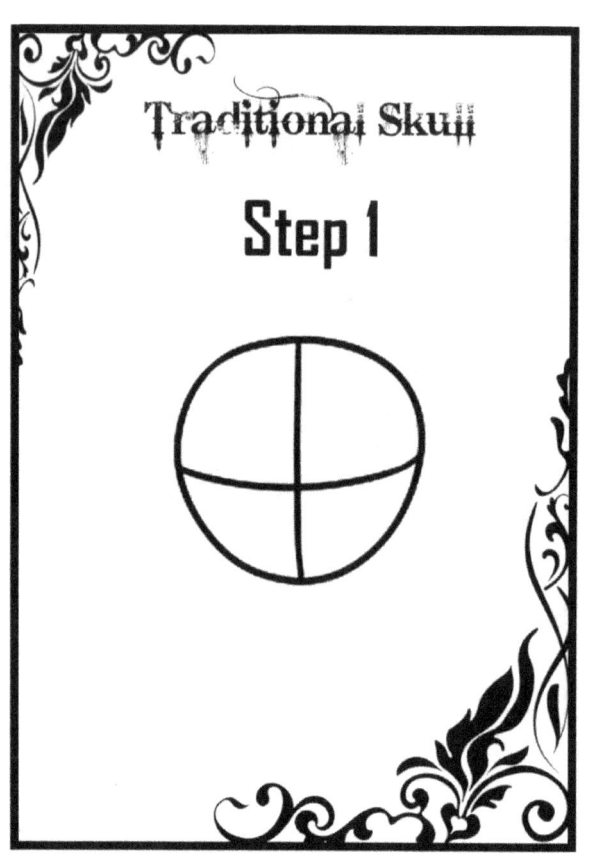

Step 2

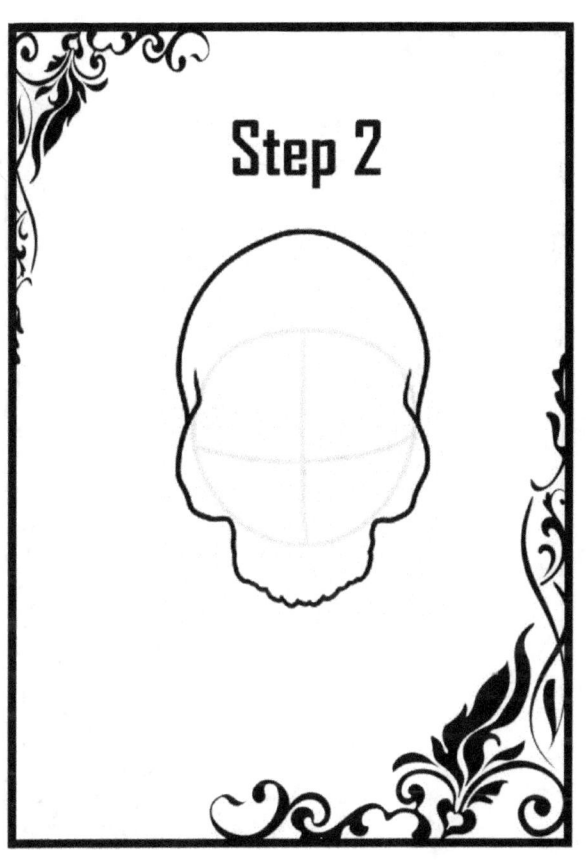

Step 3

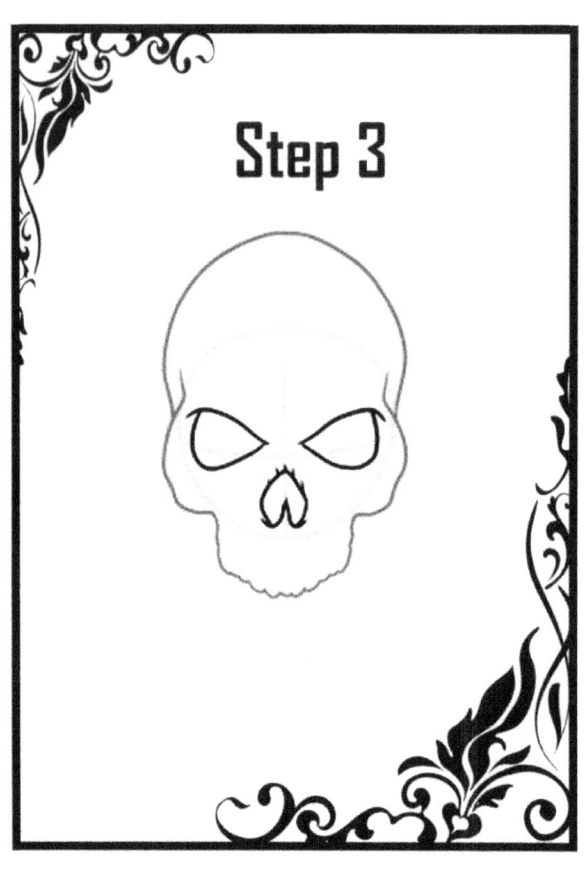

Step 4

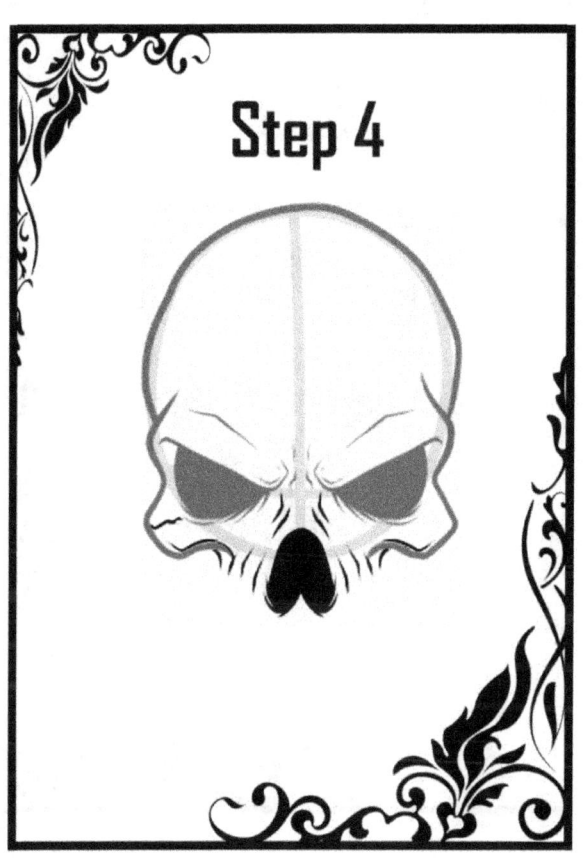

Step 5

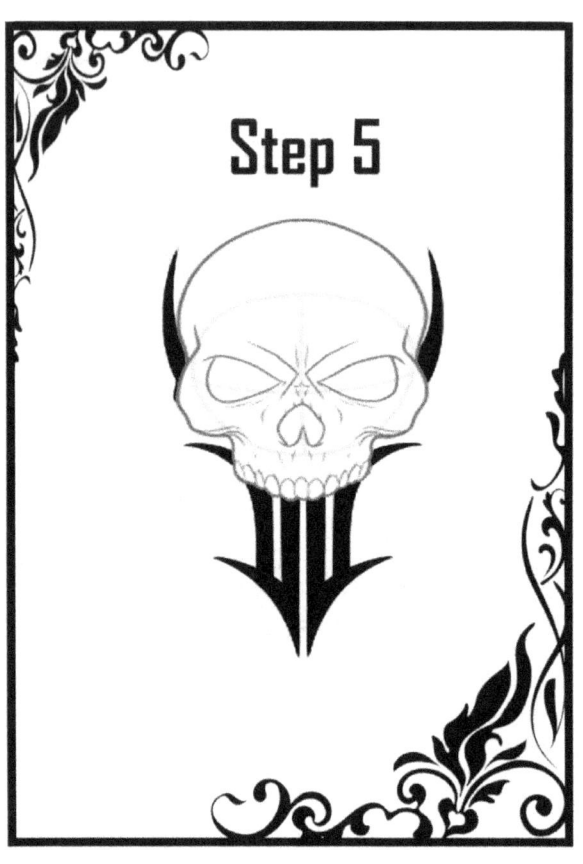

Step 6

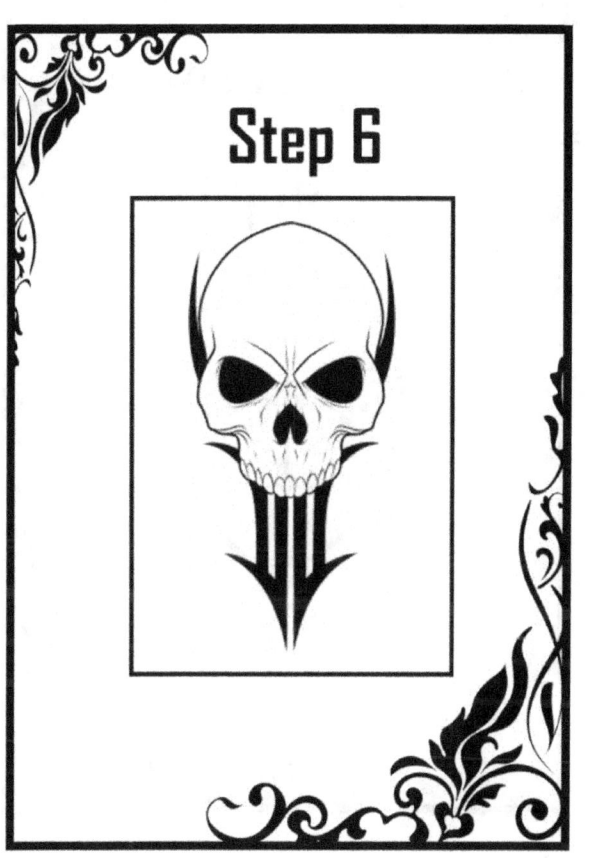

Skull And Roses

Step 1

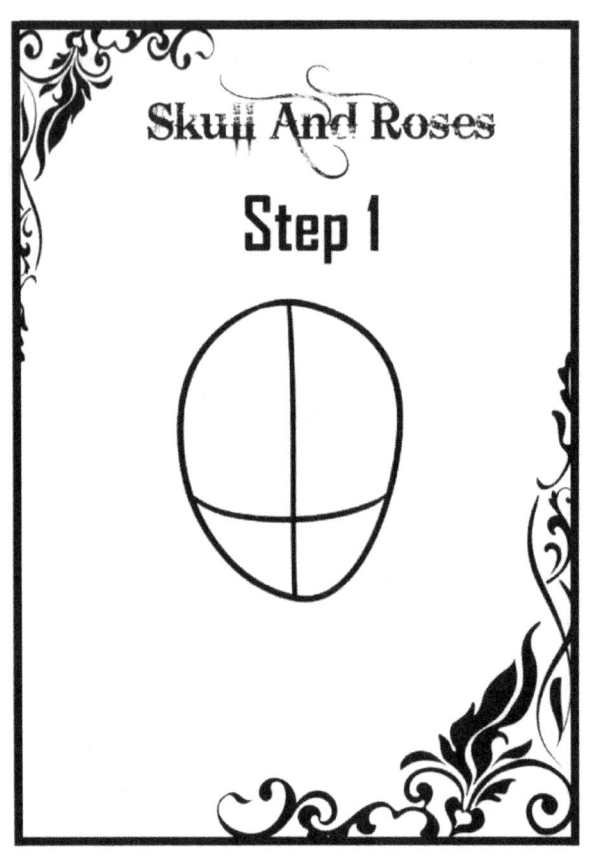

Step 2

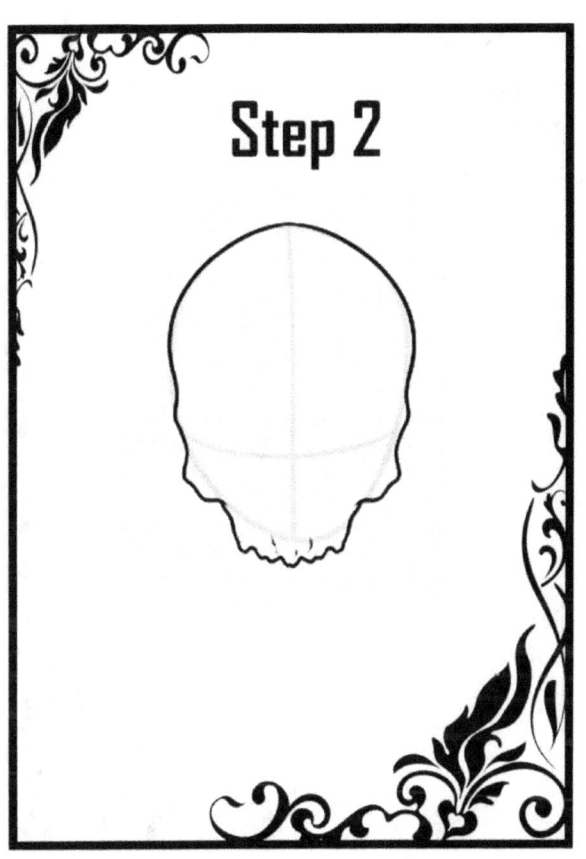

Step 3

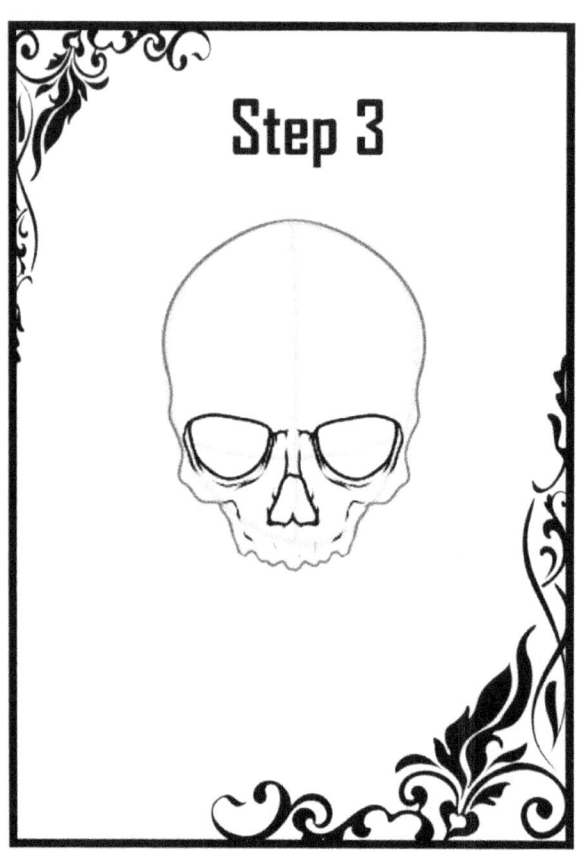

Step 4

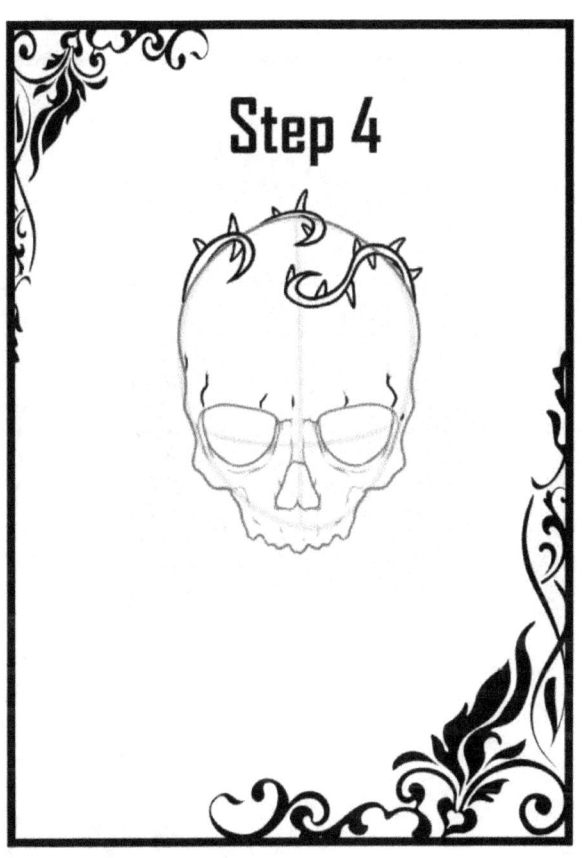

Step 5

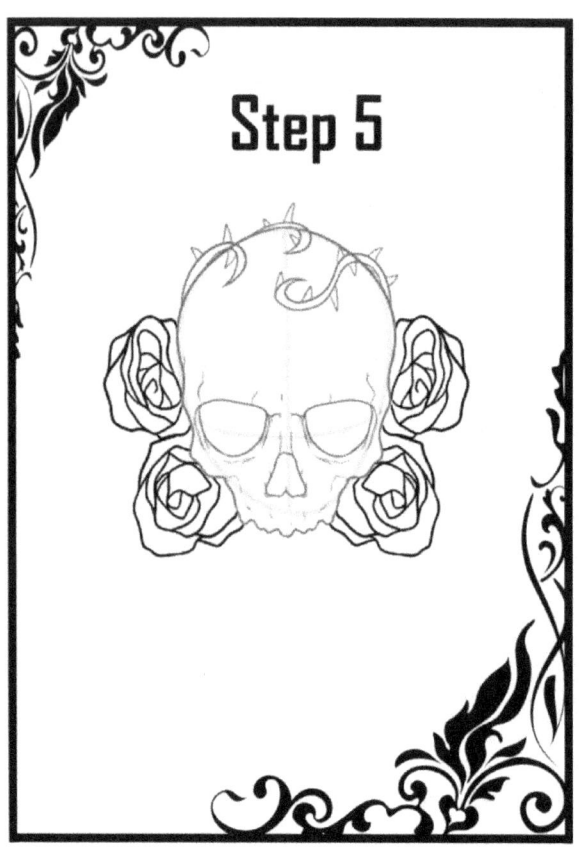

Step 6

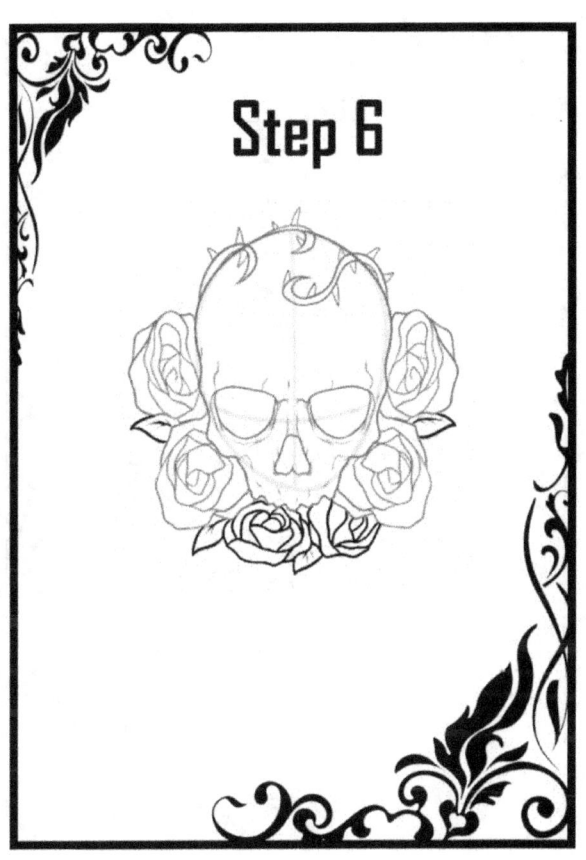

Step 7

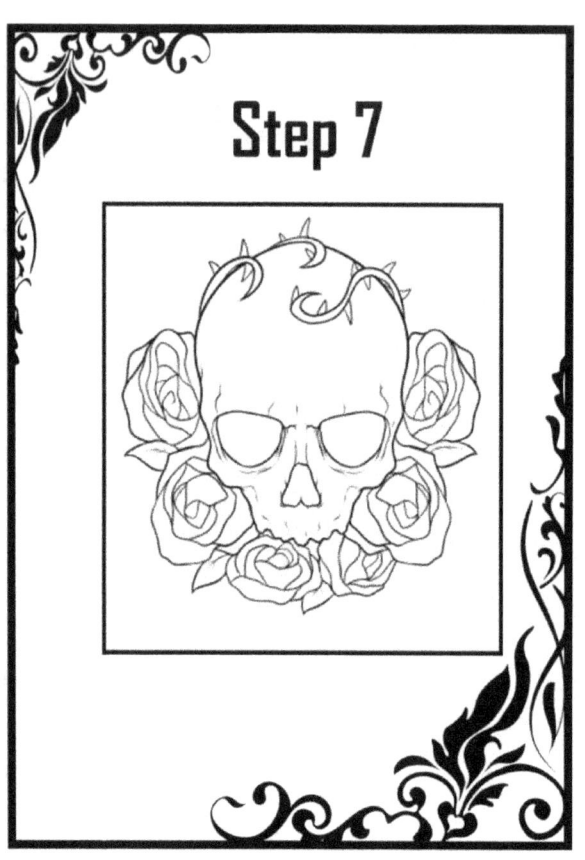